Hannah Whitall Smith

Hannah Whitall Smith

* * * * * * * * * * * * * *

MARIE HENRY

BETHANY HOUSE PUBLISHERS
MINNEAPOLIS, MINNESOTA 55438

Originally published by Chosen Books under the title *The Secret Life of Hannah Whitall Smith.*

Published by Bethany House Publishers
A Ministry of Bethany Fellowship, Inc.
6820 Auto Club Road, Minneapolis, Minnesota 55438

Printed in the United States of America

Library of Congress Cataloging-in-Publication Data

Henry, Marie.
    Hannah Whitall Smith / Marie Henry.
       p. cm.
    Rev. ed. of: The secret life of Hannah Whitall Smith

    1. Smith, Hannah Whitall, 1832–1911. 2. Quakers—Pennsylvania—Philadelphia—Biography. 3. Philadelphia (Pa.)—Biography. 4. Women, Quaker—Pennsylvania—Philadelphia—Biography.
I. Title.
BX7795.S6H45   1993
289.6'092—dc20   92–21189
[B]
ISBN 1–55661–316–4   CIP

In memory of my father

Dr. E. G. Montag

May 10, 1900—June 17, 1990

And of my sister

Betty Jo Montag

January 25, 1928—August 20, 1984

without whose help and encouragement this book

might never have been written.

I dedicate this book to my children,

Leona Denne

Second Lieutenant Len Hall

Ellen Cantrell

MARIE HENRY is an ordained Presbyterian minister living in Utah. In researching and developing the ideas for this biography, she was encouraged by Catherine Marshall, a great admirer of Hannah Whitall Smith.

Acknowledgments

I wish to express my gratitude to the late Catherine Marshall LeSourd for encouraging me in my research that formed the basis for this book. She and I exchanged many letters during 1980 and 1981. Our correspondence helped me in developing my ideas for the manuscript. Catherine was a great admirer of Hannah Whitall Smith. In many ways my book was born out of the letters Catherine and I exchanged. I also wish to thank Barbara Strachey Halpern, great-granddaughter of Hannah. Mrs. Halpern not only made all Hannah's personal letters available to me, but she also allowed me to remove the letters from her house long enough to photocopy them. In addition to this she loaned me certain papers and photographs of the Pearsall Smith family. Mrs. Halpern was most hospitable to me during the three weeks I was in Oxford, England, sorting through the Smith Archive. She offered me a room in her house rent-free and fed me gourmet meals. I can't thank Mrs. Halpern enough for her kindness and cooperation. I wish to thank Jayne Schneider of the Clifford Barbour Library of Pittsburgh Theological Seminary for being so cooperative about getting rare books relating to Hannah from inter-library loan. Many thanks go to Gary T. Mohler of Canonsburg,

Pennsylvania, for reading the original manuscript and for giving me valuable suggestions for the rewrite. Celine Cebedo typed the second draft of the manuscript, for which I thank her.

Marie Henry

Sometimes a Light Surprises

Sometimes a light surprises the Christian while he sings;
it is the Lord, who rises with healing in His wings;
when comforts are declining, He grants the soul again
a season of clear shining to cheer it after rain.

In holy contemplation we sweetly then pursue
the theme of God's salvation, and find it ever new;
set free from present sorrow, we cheerfully can say,
let the unknown tomorrow bring with it what it may.

It can bring with it nothing but He will bear us through;
who gives the lilies clothing will clothe His people too;
beneath the spreading heavens no creature but is fed;
and He who feeds the ravens will give His children bread.

Though vine nor fig tree neither their wonted fruit shall
    bear,
though all the field should wither nor flocks nor herds be
    there;
yet God the same abiding, His praise shall tune my voice,
for while in Him confiding I cannot but rejoice.

William Cowper, 1779

Contents

Light in the Darkness

Families today are assaulted by an epidemic of troubles. Even the most devout families are sometimes shaken by divorce, problems with children, career disappointments, unresolved bitterness in relationships, illness that won't go away.

As a result, more and more people are turning to faith and spirituality for answers. Unfortunately, a prevailing notion has grown among many believers that if you are living a life of faith and obedience and surrender, God will supernaturally remove all difficulty and pain. The wayward son will suddenly embrace Christ; the unbelieving husband will have some spiritual experience that turns him into a thoughtful, considerate lover; the chronic disease will be cured.

The truth is that for many faithful believers their unpleasant life circumstances are not dramatically changed. Trouble and pain can go on and on. As a result many Christians question their faith and wonder if God has simply left them in the dark.

These battered Christians of the twentieth century need some encouragement, some reinforcement, someone to say, "It's all right if your troubles and pain don't vanish miraculously. It doesn't mean that your faith is lacking, or that your walk with Christ is somehow suspect. Some of the real stalwarts of the faith also had to keep going in blind obedience as disappointment followed heartbreak in their personal lives."

It is that kind of reassurance this biography of Hannah Whitall Smith attempts to bring. Many devoted readers of her books may imagine her as a sweet old lady in quaint Quaker garb, who spent her life in some kind of sheltered rose garden. The truth is that this writer of the best-selling Christian classic *The Christian's Secret of a Happy Life* had some agonizing experiences with members of her family and went through periods of great discouragement, doubt, and even despair.

Because Hannah did not receive the outward blessings that seemed due such a devout Christian, Christian publishers have shunned doing her biography. I feel that her story is all the more triumphant because she was not rewarded for her devoutness.

Still other publishers have chosen to ignore the facts of her life because of one doctrine she came to believe. That was Hannah's belief that God, because He is love, will make a way for even the worst sinner to be reconciled to himself in the end, which was known in her day as the doctrine of "restitution"; and her hope in this act of ultimate love on God's part made her controversial in her own lifetime. And so, many Christians do not know how to account for this embarrassing flirtation with what we now call "universalism"—they choose to overlook it, much as they overlook its presence in lives of other great Christian writers of that era, such as George MacDonald. Before I say more about Hannah's influence on me during the darkest time of my life, it's important to put this element of Hannah's beliefs in context.

Most contemporary readers are unaware how strongly the doctrine of "predestination" gripped much of the church in the nineteenth century. This belief teaches that

God has chosen certain people to love and enjoy Him both in this life and in the world to come—just as He has chosen to "predestine" others for an eternity in hellfire. In denominations that held this view strictly, some were even told—the poet Emily Dickinson, for example—that they were definitely among the lost, beyond any hope of salvation. This occasioned one of Dickinson's most poignant lyric "prayers," which starts: *Why do they shut me out of heaven?**

To put it simply, Hannah—so expansive in her inner being—was, first and foremost, overwhelmed by the vast love of God, so much so that she could see nothing but His kindness and mercy. More important, she could see His goodness in all things, even the earthly events that seem so terrible to us: God only allowed "bad" things to happen to His children so they would learn to leave off seeking security in temporal things and to turn their hearts to Him. And so, to Hannah, even the fires of hell would not be everlasting, but would be a final, terrible discipline for those with exceedingly hard hearts, used to break through their utter spiritual darkness and set them free at some far distant point in eternity to bow the knee to Jesus Christ.

So, it was Hannah's recoil from the sterile sternness of "predestination," coupled with her boundless love for her own children, that made her turn to her God whose tender mercies toward His children were unending. In the end, as we shall see, note her mistake in being too lovingly lax with her children: There is no way to fix exactly what she believed about "restitution" when she came to the end of her days.

This theological issue set aside for the time being, what is it about Hannah's writing that has drawn Christians to its light for more than a century?

It was Hannah's pain-filled experiences that attracted me to her. Back in 1967, after I had experienced a life-

---

*See *The Complete Poems of Emily Dickinson*, edited by Thomas H. Johnson; Little, Brown. #248.

changing encounter with Christ, a dear Christian woman in a prayer group I was attending handed me two little books by Hannah Whitall Smith, a Quaker woman of the nineteenth century. Later, when I tried to read one of them, it seemed to have nothing to offer me.

Odd, but just at the moment a person would expect one's life to be flooded with new blessings, mine began to go from disaster to disaster. My husband and I separated, then were divorced. There was much upheaval in our school district and I lost my job as a schoolteacher. In the summer of 1972, my three children and I left California and traveled to New York, where I looked for another teaching job.

When no positions were available, I found myself back in school at the age of 37, studying full time for the pastoral ministry at Pittsburgh Theological Seminary. In 1976 I graduated from this seminary and was ordained as one of the 350-some women ministers in the United Presbyterian Church. Then came part-time work as an area field minister in a rural parish in southwest Pennsylvania. But this job was frustrating and disappointing. I became depressed, frightened, and suffered a partial breakdown.

At this low period in my life I noticed the dusty paperback books by Hannah Whitall Smith that had been stowed among my other goods since 1967. I opened the first volume, called *God of All Comfort*, and began to read. Though she wrote this book at a time when she was beset with all manner of difficulties, Hannah had a message of God's tender love and care that fell like life-giving rain on my dry soul. I read the second book, *Everyday Religion*, and then went out and purchased the most famous of Hannah's books, *The Christian's Secret of a Happy Life*. A great curiosity about the woman who had written these books grew in me. Personally, it was like finding a light after stumbling in darkness for a long way.

Learning that Catherine Marshall LeSourd had been a devoted follower of Mrs. Smith, I wrote to her seeking more information on Hannah's life. A correspondence developed between us as I began to explore with her the possibility of writing a biography of the fascinating nineteenth-century author, preacher, and advocate of a woman's right to vote.

Since I had access to the Clifford Barbour Library of Pittsburgh Theological Seminary, I was able to order obscure books related to Hannah Smith through inter-library loan. One of her books, *The Spiritual Autobiography*, was such a rare volume that I photocopied the whole book.

I discovered that additional unpublished material was in the possession of Barbara Strachey Halpern, Hannah's great-granddaughter, who lived in Oxford, England. Then, through correspondence with Mrs. Halpern, I learned that she had in her possession the Smith Archive, which contains some 6,000 letters written by Hannah, plus 12 volumes of her journals.

In January 1982 I flew to London and, at the personal invitation of Mrs. Halpern, spent three and a half weeks going through the Smith Archive, photocopying some 875 pages of letters and recording hours of material from the journals on tape.

These letters, excerpts from the journals, and the published material I had already researched form the basis of this biography—the story of a life that few know, but one that can bring new hope and spiritual light to hurting people today.

This is my prayer.

Marie Henry
Kanab, Utah
May 1992

1

The Sugar-Scoop Bonnet

On a wintery day late in 1848, the congregation of the 12th Street Quaker Meetinghouse in Philadelphia was gathered to pay its respects to God. The meetinghouse was a plain, bare room with wooden, uncushioned benches. Outside the tall uncurtained windows, a gray sky looked as dull as the meeting's interior and the colorless clothes of the faithful.

A complete stillness pervaded the whole meeting. Not even a child would dare to disturb the stillness, for every boy and girl had been rigorously taught not to swing their legs, fidget, or make a sound while the faithful were meditating. At the front of the room were plain benches on a raised platform. Along these benches sat the "ministers," men and women with no formal theological training who had been singled out as possessing special gifts of discernment and prophecy. In the silence, they listened for a message from God.

Down among the congregation, the men and boys sat on one side, their quiet Quaker garb blending in with the whitewashed walls and the unfinished woodwork of the rough benches. On the other side of the chilly room the women and girls remained absolutely still, heads bowed.

Their plain dresses, like their husbands' cutaway coats, breeches, and broad-brimmed hats, were all in neutral shades. No trace of color could be seen, except in the pale flesh tones of the faces of the worshipers.

After a good forty-five minutes of silence, a man in a charcoal-gray long coat, one of the "ministers," suddenly stood up. Rows of pale faces turned up expectantly at the leader as he began to speak. His harsh, resonating voice spilled out over the room, reverberating from the bare walls.

"God has given me a message," the minister began. "I have noticed among the young ladies of our meeting that too few have put on a plain bonnet. I see among our younger women examples of the frivolities of worldly people." He paused. "I have even seen gold watches and neck pins, jewelry with which the plain people of God should not adorn themselves."

Pointing a finger toward the ladies' side of the meeting, his eyes blazed like that of an Old Testament prophet.

"I believe that the Lord has given me a message for some young heart present," he continued. "God has called her to take up her cross, to put on plain dress, to burn her gold breast pins and any other adornments that she may possess, to give up immediately any beloved possessions that she may cherish too greatly."

The air of conviction could be felt around the room, for Quakers believed that the Holy Spirit spoke directly from the mouth of their ministers; the congregation regarded the speaker as the very oracle of God. His words brought color to the cheeks of at least two of the girls sitting sedately with their female relations. One was a young woman with a vivid face and luxuriant blonde hair that was only partly covered by her straw cottage bonnet. She stared at the preacher with unmistakable horror. Lowering her head, she secretly reached for her shirt front, where a small and beautifully crafted gold watch hung on a chain around her neck. With two fingers she felt the disk of metal, then slipped it inside her dress where it could not be seen. Silently she prayed, *Dear God, my father gave me this gold watch only last week. Please—let the message not be for me.*

The girl was Hannah Whitall.* She was an intelligent, even brilliant young woman of 16, with a zestful approach toward life—which only partially concealed a rebellious attitude toward the restrictions of her Quaker family. But Hannah was an uncomfortable rebel, and beneath her outward resistance lay a deep sensitivity and a curiosity about things of the Spirit.

Another young woman was stricken by the Quaker preacher that morning, too. A few rows in front of Hannah, stiff and straight, sat one of her friends, Abby Blackwood. The minister's fiery words had done their job, so penetrating Abby's heart that she began to sob uncontrollably.

Even when the meeting closed and the faithful began to disband, Abby remained in her seat. She could not stop the tears. One of the elders, noticing her emotion, made her way to Abby's side. "Precious child, I believe the Lord has spoken to thee. Mayest thou be obedient to the heavenly vision."†

Both Hannah and Abby would return home that day with the heavy words of their pastor weighing on their spirits.

Since Mr. and Mrs. Blackwood were away on a trip, Abby plodded the sidewalks of Philadelphia back to the house that was quiet but for the unobtrusive presence of a few servants. The conviction would not leave: The Lord had spoken to her through the preacher, and she was to destroy all her cherished possessions. Abby cried on her bed for a while. Then with sudden determination she rose. Heavy-hearted, she pulled out of her wardrobe several dresses—two in silk with ribbon and ruffles, a summery muslin with

---

*Pronounced White-all.

†Author's note: I have retained the old Quaker "thee" and "thou" in much of the conversation throughout this book in deference to Hannah Smith's strong convictions that the pure Quaker speech be preserved.

a pink flowered print—also her lace-edged drawers and a blue velvet bonnet trimmed with matching feathers. Like a sleepwalker, she reached for her jewelry box and took out her pearl and ruby-studded gold pins and her gold thimble. Gathering up her bundle, she carried it downstairs. Gritting her teeth in pain, she lifted down from the wall her most prized possession, a painting she had done in water colors, a beautiful scene that her parents so loved they had it framed.

Placing her clothes and her jewelry on top of the picture, she built up the fire in the big living room fireplace until it was a roaring blaze. One by one she fed her small mound of treasures to the flames. "Oh, God help me," she said over and over, as she watched her beloved belongings turn to charred ruins.

"Oh, God, I have done it," she whispered. "I have been faithful to thy will."

Abby returned to her empty house, alone. But there was no joy or freedom in her offering, only the weighty sense of a spiritual "duty completed." Her spirit felt broken.[1] From then on, Abby decided she *would* accept the plain clothes and that dreaded emblem of Quaker sanctity, the ugly sugar-scoop bonnet.

Only a few blocks away, the Whitall family had returned to their residence after the meeting: parents, Mary and John Whitall; Hannah, 16; her sister Sarah (called Sally), 15; James, 14; and Mary, 12. The hush and awe of the Quaker Meeting had weighed down their spirits, too.

Their home, on quiet Filbert Street, was spacious and simple. No paintings decorated the walls. No mirrors were to be seen. The furniture was simple and functional. The plainest of white curtains hung at the windows. No ornaments or knickknacks were in evidence, nor were there any novels, works of art, or musical instruments. These were all considered worldly distractions, and the Whitalls were noted at the meeting for having a proper Quaker home. Though John Whitall's flourishing glass factory was quite prosperous, there was not a sign of opulence in this stark bare and painfully clean house, presided over by Mary Whitall.

Like her friend Abby, Hannah Whitall had also quailed inwardly at the message that morning. Part of her felt drawn to the sacrificial element in it, but a strong love of life in her rebelled. She hated the large, obscuring bonnet—the "sugar-scoop"—that became part of the uniform of every Quaker woman who denied herself. Hannah loved beauty. She was drawn to the elegant clothes displayed in Philadelphia's finer women's shops. And her boundless curiosity about the world made her resist the constricting thought of giving up all fun things in order to be "good."

———

The following May, when Hannah was seventeen, she did a daring and forbidden thing. She stole away one morning and slipped inside the cool marbled halls of the Philadelphia Academy of the Fine Arts.

Later, she burst into her home like a mini-hurricane in long dove-colored skirts, and kissed her sweet-faced mother on the cheek. Then she whirled and danced about the living room.

"Thee must learn to show some ladylike restraint," said Mary Whitall quietly. Would her daughter never calm down?

Hannah could not repress her enthusiasm. "Mother, I cannot help it. The grass is so green, the trees are just putting forth their leaves. And I'm aware of how numberless are my blessings!" She began to chuckle. "And besides, the laugh is in me and must come out."

With this, Hannah ran lightly up the stairs.[2]

Upstairs she barged into the bedroom of her sister Sally. "Thee must hear what I did today, Sally—a dreadful, forbidden thing. Can thee keep a secret?"

"We have always shared things," Sally replied from where she was seated on her bed. She was more quiet and serious than her ebullient older sister, and deeply devoted to her.

Hannah shut the door stealthily and sat down on the quilt, next to Sally. She began in a whisper. "Thee knows, Sally, that I have always had a great desire to visit the Philadelphia Academy of the Fine Arts."

"But, Sister," Sally interrupted, "we Friends avoid such snares of the devil—music and dancing and pictures."

"Yes, I know," Hannah went on hastily, "but I had to go just once. So today I went inside. My heart was beating so hard and my mouth was so dry. I know it was perilously wicked, but I had to see. I went by the pictures so quickly that everything was a blur. Then I saw the statue—would thee believe, a marble group with Hero and Leander. And Sally, Leander had no clothes on! My heart was in my mouth and I was thinking, *I suppose I shall go straight to hell, but I will look at this statue.* And I knew what a daring sinner I was and I gathered up my skirts and flew outside."

Hannah lay back on her sister's bed and stared wide-eyed at the ceiling. Sally's eyes were fixed grimly on her errant sister. "Once I was in the open air," Hannah went on. "I stopped and leaned against a pillar until I caught my breath. I was just sure that God would send a lightning bolt out of heaven and strike me dead.[3] But nothing happened and I walked home. The birds were singing and the trees were budding. It was such a lovely day; the sun was shining and everything was bursting forth in new life. By the time I got home, I wasn't fearful anymore."

"Oh, Hannah," Sally remonstrated, shaking her head sorrowfully, "will thee tell Mother?"

"No, I shall not tell Mother," said Hannah resolutely. "It would only worry her. And remember—thee promised to keep this a secret."

And with this, Hannah charged off to her own bedroom to tidy herself for the evening meal.

Later that night, Hannah dressed in her nightgown and prepared for bed. Then she lit the stubs of three candles and pulled a small leather-covered book from her desk drawer. It was *Volume II* of a journal that Hannah had been keeping for a year now. Its pages held evidence that the nighttime Hannah could be much different from the adventurous daytime Hannah. Bleak thoughts came to her about the state of her soul, thoughts that would never have intruded in the sunlight. This night, as was her habit, Hannah sat down at her desk. Hannah was unaware of Abby's actions after the meeting. She dipped her quill in the inkwell and wrote:

I have been so rebellious. I have so entirely neglected prayer and felt so little sorrow of heart on account of it that I cannot but believe that God has left me to myself. I know well my utter desolation without a Savior.

Tears had come to her eyes. She rubbed at them with the sleeve of her nightgown. Then she went: *My mind entirely acknowledges my own worthlessness and my need of a redeemer. Oh, if my heavenly Father does not help me I shall indeed be lost.*[4] In this manner, she poured out other morose and despairing thoughts until drowsiness made her head swim.

The 1840s passed into the 1850s as life went on smoothly in the Whitall household. John Whitall's business at the glass factory continued to prosper, while Mary provided a comfortable haven for the four children.

The conflict was far from over in Hannah's high-strung young spirit. This world's life had such an allure. She adored the new fashions. And she all but lived to gallop freely over open farmlands on her horse, Rollo. With the sun and wind on her face—what a beautiful world it was!

But wasn't a true Christian supposed to be solemn, pious at all times? Deep within, Hannah wanted to be a true Christian—someday.

On February 17, 1850, Hannah, just turned eighteen, was sitting sedately in the Friends' meeting, her face a mask of dutiful piety. Inside, as usual, thoughts were churning. *Wouldn't it be wonderful if in some unaccountable manner I should become perfectly good? I should dress like Mother in a cap and handkerchief, with a sugar-scoop bonnet and hooded cloak and should preach at the very next meeting I attended. I would be so magnificently eloquent, so grandly sublime. And then I would go on a religious visit to England, where the whole nation, even the queen herself, would crowd to hear the young, eloquent Quaker girl.*[5]

Hannah sighed, imagining a further preaching tour to France. But her grandiose vision was cut short by the closing of the meeting—and there she was again, plain Hannah Whitall, who had never received any signs of heavenly favor and who could not bring herself to give up her gold watch or her new silk dress.

Since her mid-teens, Hannah had been seesawing back and forth between the demands of piety and the desires of her fun-loving nature. There seemed to be some invisible wall preventing her from the act that her expansive and impulsive nature would have her do—to throw herself passionately and headlong into a life of serving God. But God seemed so stern-faced and unhappy, so harshly demanding. Why had He created so beautiful and bright a world; and why fill a young woman with such unbridled joy in living if He thought this world was so thoroughly dark and life so soured by sin, as the ministers claimed? In the simple goodness of life, and in the sweet loveliness of the world, Hannah's soul found comfort and light. She could not pretend she found these things distasteful. It would be a lie. Was there something her spiritual elders were missing? Or was it that she herself would never be able—as she sometimes thought in her more dour moments alone—to come to God?

In November 1850, a life-changing event took place, something ordinary in the life of a young woman. Who could know it would soon alter her course forever? Robert Pearsall Smith came a-courting. Robert was in every way a desirable suitor: age 24, handsome and gifted and, like herself, a birthright Quaker. Throughout the spring of 1851, the fervent Robert sent Hannah notes—and a special bouquet of flowers picked from the garden of the little cottage in Germantown, Pennsylvania, that he had rented as their future home. Attached to the bouquet was a passionate little note: *Mayest thou live to enjoy many beautiful flowers and happy hours there as my bride, my friend, my congenial companion and ardently loved (may I say it?) wife.*[6] Being courted by Robert was like being swept into the middle of a romantic novel, full of poetry, moonlight, and roses.

Hannah was also charmed by her fiancé's high-minded attitudes. He told her that he never passed five minutes without considering what was right. Robert was a sensitive, devout young man, full of idealistic visions about their married life together. They spent much time in solemn discussion about their religious duties and their mutual longing for spiritual growth. Robert wrote to her, *Having come thus far on our way, do not let us, my dearest friend, be discouraged but press on for the mark of the prize of our high calling in Christ. Enable me, oh my Savior, to live today as in thy sight.*[7]

Robert's extreme piety and rhetoric exerted a sobering effect on his beloved. Hannah became more serious, quieter, and tried to be docile. Her frivolity was toned down by his insistence on strict Quaker observances all throughout their formal and carefully supervised courtship. And as for Hannah's parents, little was said to her about sexual love or about conflict in marriage: All instruction was focused on her Christian duties as a suitable "helpmeet" for her husband. Robert was so devout, and Hannah felt blessed to have been chosen by such a man. Could she ever begin to match his seeming faith and devotion?

Robert and Hannah were married on November 5, 1851. A honeymoon radiance pervaded Hannah's spirit as this

19-year-old bride moved quite happily into the little home in Germantown and began married life as the proud wife of Robert Pearsall Smith.

There was no way anyone could have prophesied that this high-spirited, carefree girl would become one of the most widely read and significant Christian writers of her time. Or that her bouyant spirit would go through a long and excruciating period of testing. Or that the triumphant faith she was to write about would be challenged in a Job-like series of personal tragedies.

2

A Blaze of Inner Light

The early years of Robert and Hannah's marriage were fairly normal, but difficult ones. Hannah became pregnant soon after the ceremony. Since the mortality rate for women in childbirth was very high in the mid-nineteenth century, most expectant mothers struggled with morbid thoughts of death.

On July 22, 1852, Hannah wrote in her journal: *Oh, my precious Savior, who died that I might live in thee. This may be the last entry I shall make in this book.*[1]

By August 10, she safely delivered a baby girl. Formally, the child was named Eleanor, but she would always be called Nellie or Ella. By 1854, Hannah was pregnant again and quite upset about it, since she and Robert had agreed that there were to be no more children for a while. Little Frank was born in the summer of 1854.

The years 1854–1858 were times of intense inner struggle for the young mother. The needs of her two children took much of her time. Robert's publishing business kept him away a great deal. He commuted to and from Philadelphia each day on horse-drawn tram cars. The marriage was solid, although Hannah's sexually repressed upbringing may have contributed to the periods of moody depression Robert experienced. Or was something deeper troubling him, something overlooked in the thrill of courtship?

Hannah's journal became even more important to her as an emotional outlet. On its pages she poured out all her religious doubts. One afternoon in early November 1856, Hannah was sitting at a table by the window of the little parlor in the Germantown house. Both children were napping. She tried to set aside this hour each day to review her spiritual progress or setbacks.

Much of her confusion was over the nature of God, which she had struggled with most of her early life. The sense of separation from God and an inability to relate to Him became a torment. *I [feel] myself cut off from God entirely*, she confided to the stark pages. *I [feel] like a sinking boat, tossed about by a mighty tempest on the godless deep of life, listening with anguished ears to the falling away of its ever breaking shore. I no longer trust God. If God was good, why did He make human beings who are so naturally inclined to evil and so averse to good? I . . . wonder if God could be all-powerful, since the creatures He created seem to have so little power to resist evil. . . .*

At least I am not now in such a totally hopeless spiritual state as I was last year. There must be a good and merciful and loving spirit somewhere in the universe. This spirit could not look upon man, fallen and miserable as he is, without yearning to save him from the awful fate toward which his own nature, or some powerful fiend, constantly and almost irresistibly urges him. Consequently, there must be a Savior.[2]

During this time, Hannah not only questioned God's permissiveness toward evil, but also the reality of her own beliefs. She wondered if she could get closer to God by giving up her jewelry, dressing in plain clothing, and adopting the sugar-scoop bonnet. But when she prayed to God about this, no answer came.

She was coming to one conclusion, however, that would have serious consequences. The Quaker meetings did not meet her spiritual needs or answer her questions. What she dreaded was the suffering emotions and the persecution that would come upon her if she were to resign from Quaker Meeting. Since almost all her family, relatives, and friends were Quakers, her resignation would grieve them beyond belief. Still she was determined to seek the truth and to pray that she might abide by it.

In March of 1857, Robert and Hannah were sitting close to the big fireplace in their front parlor on a sleety late-winter evening. On the table between them an oil lamp flickered. Hannah presented to her husband another subject that was beginning to lie heavily on her mind.

"Robert," she began intensely, "I am dismayed at what downright simpletons most women are! When I walk along the street, I feel I would like to give every woman I meet a good shaking! Dress—fudge! Gossip—worse still. And that is really the extent of their conversation. Most women and men today feel that women are incapable of developing our minds. We are kept in a state of perpetual childhood."[3] She looked anxiously over at Robert to see how he was reacting to these revolutionary thoughts.

"Thee is right," he said surprisingly as he got up to heave another log onto the already blazing flame. "But do wives and mothers have the time to pursue further education?"

"Yes, they do," replied Hannah. And she launched into a vigorous description of how she and her close friends felt about the state of affairs between men and women. Because women were expected to be a sort of extension of their husbands, they often considered themselves inferior human beings. Robert listened patiently, surprising Hannah with his understanding.

After a long discussion, Robert agreed to hire a tutor to help prepare Hannah for entrance into the junior class at Haverford College. A governess could help superintend the children. He said they might even move to Haverford so that Hannah could live at home until graduation. Hannah was ecstatic.

A month later, however, she reluctantly abandoned her ambitious plans to be a college student primarily because she feared she would have to neglect her children. Instead, a tutor began coming regularly to Hannah's home to advance her education.

Then came a blow that would send the family reeling. By December 1857, the family had moved from Germantown to Philadelphia to be closer to Robert's publishing work. They had only just settled into their new house on 220 North 10th Street when five-year-old Nellie took sick with a bronchial infection.

Christmas was only a few days away, but there was no gaiety in the Smith household. Hannah and Robert took turns sitting beside the fevered body of their little daughter. There was little they could do except sponge the small flushed face with cool water. Nellie lay so still, she seemed almost like a small waxen doll.

The night of December 22 was bitterly cold and cloud-covered. Silent tears ran unchecked down the young mother's face. A flood of memories engulfed her: Nellie's sweet voice singing the Jesus songs Hannah had taught her; Nellie's soft hands stroking her face; Nellie's clear, sweet voice saying her prayers.

The hours passed on through that bleak night. Robert appeared several times to spell his wife. Then toward dawn the tiny spark of life in Nellie slowly flickered out.

Five days later Nellie Smith was buried in the family cemetery at Laurel Hill. A pale winter sun shone down as the small procession made its way to the graveside. The horses that had drawn the funeral carriage paced nervously in the background, chomping in the frosty air. The pall-bearers carried the small casket to where a shallow hole had been hacked in the frozen ground. Snow covered the grass lightly and fringed all the branches of the trees. Hannah and Robert, soberly clad in Quaker-dark, stood with wooden faces and watched as the casket was lowered into its shallow depression. The still air bore the soft sounds of weeping. And all the time the small group of mourners stood beside the child's grave, a small bird on a branch, right over Hannah's head, sang a quiet little song.[4]

Hannah held up fairly well through the burial service.

The next day, grief overwhelmed her.

Pacing her little parlor in anguish, she cried out to her husband, "Nellie looked so beautiful in death that I felt almost comforted. But now—oh, the bitterness and loneliness I feel. My daughter, my daughter!"[5]

Death was a fact of life in the 1850s. Hardly a single family escaped without the loss of a budding young life. Childhood diseases carried off the young and fragile: scarlet fever, typhoid, lung disease. Medicine in the mid-nineteenth century had no defense against these cruel killers of the young. A mother in 1857 could not expect all of her children to grow up to be adults.

Nevertheless, Nellie's death left Hannah nearly inconsolable. Her journal on February 2 recorded: *My heart is ready to burst at the thought of my sweet, gentle, loving daughter; the arch look out of her bright eyes when she was meditating a piece of fun; the matronly expression of her childish face as she stood washing her little dresses or putting her sick dolly to bed.*[6]

Strange to say, but it was through the cloud of darkness surrounding Hannah that a small bright ray of spiritual light began to shine. For the first time in the two years since Hannah had openly questioned her beliefs, she felt a sense of God's presence. The memory of Nellie's innocent faith encouraged her to strive earnestly after holiness. From deep inside, she called out to her daughter, "My precious child, my angel child, thou shalt indeed be, I trust, a link to draw me up to heaven."[7]

And so the winter would pass, and the faint promise of spring pressed from the tips of bare branches.

When the Pearsall Smith family vacationed at the seashore in Atlantic City during the summer of 1858, Hannah decided to take along no book but the Bible. She was determined to deal with her lingering resentment toward God. Day after day she sat in her chair on the beach, poring over Scripture texts. One warm, cloudless day in early September she was reading on the beach, the only sounds being the distant laughter of little children building a sand castle and the sea gulls whirling and cawing above her. Then it happened.

She had turned to chapter five of the book of Romans and her weeks of search for God's truth were suddenly rewarded. Verse eight blazed forth at her: "While we were yet sinners, Christ died for us." She closed her Bible and, lying back in her chair, shut her eyes. The wonder of the salvation that comes through Jesus suffused her whole being. A healing, comforting peace warmed her whole being—something she had never felt the like of before.

After all my years of rebellion and unbelief, my Savior still had compassion on me and has revealed himself to me. Oh, the fullness and the freshness of His grace. I can say in truth that I would not exchange the salvation which is freely given by Christ for all the righteousness which years of perfect obedience to the law could win for me. I know now that I don't have to wear a sugar-scoop bonnet to please God. Christ has done it all for me on the cross. His sacrifice is all I need to be restored to right relationship with God. I don't have to keep trying to win God's favor with fruitless efforts to be "good." While I was yet a sinner, Christ died for me. Could anything be more liberating than that?[8]

It was as if her image of the demanding and punitive God had cracked. If He could feel the hurt of a mother in her loss, if He would somehow touch her pain with His invisible and comforting hand, then He must not be the cold and aloof being others had made Him out to be.

These thoughts she later recorded. But that day, as Hannah rose from her beach chair still clutching her Bible, something in her whole being was transformed.

Raising her face to the warmth of the sun, she said exultantly, out loud: "I believe, oh, Lord, I believe!" Feeling as if she were walking on air, she picked up her beach chair and floated back to their rented lodging, anxious to share her newfound revelation with her family.

3

Family Split

As a Quaker, Hannah had been taught to listen to the inner voice for guidance. She never received any doctrinal teaching, for the Bible was often read but seldom interpreted. To a Quaker, "a concern" coming from the inner voice was considered to have more authority than the Bible. The Bible, after all, was God's voice of long ago; while the "concern" was His voice at the present moment, and as such it was of far greater importance.[1]

Thus it came as a perfect blaze of illumination to Hannah when she made her summer-long search through the Scriptures and discovered that the Bible declared that Christ alone was her salvation. Since Christ bore her sins on the cross, she did not have to placate God by dressing in dreary clothes or by struggling to improve her character. The Word of God declared that she was already right in His sight because of the free gift of grace. For Hannah, this awareness of salvation was like lifting a curtain in the land of shadows and stepping into a fair, new country.

Being Hannah, she brimmed over with her spiritual discoveries to friends and acquaintances. In the fall of 1858, any stray soul who wandered unsuspecting over the threshold of the Smiths' house was bound to be buttonholed by a zealous Hannah. The Bible was an unending source of illumination for her, and every day seemed to bring new insight, the glimpse of some new truth. She could not get enough of it. Robert was greatly affected by Hannah's obvious joy, and he too found new spiritual dimensions as they began to attend other churches.

Several months later, on a particularly blustery Sunday in January 1859, Hannah and Robert were sitting at their dining-room table after the midday meal. In the adjacent kitchen they could hear the pots and pans rattling as their servant girl prepared to wash up the dishes. Four-year-old Frank had been taken upstairs by the nursery governess and was being put to bed for his nap. Icicles fringed the windows as Hannah stared outside at the frozen garden, where the dead stalks of her summer flowers stuck up through the light carpet of snow that had fallen during the night.

"Robert," Hannah began, ending the quiet reverie, "since we have given this matter much prayerful consideration, are we agreed that we must resign our membership in the Society of Friends?"

Robert nodded. "I don't see how we can remain Friends when we feel so strongly that we must be baptized as the Bible says we should. If only the Friends did not deny the sacraments of Baptism and the Lord's Supper to their practicing members!"*

Hannah's eyes filled with pain. "It's a radical step, to think about leaving the Society. It will bring great sorrow to our families. Mine more than thine."

"Yes," Robert answered somberly. "Thy parents will put up quite a fuss. And thy brother and brothers-in-law also."

Hannah's sister Sarah was 25 years old and had been married for several years to William Nicholson, a staunch Quaker. Sister Mary was already a mother at age 22. A few

---

*Author's note: The conservative branch of Quakerism to which the Whitalls and Smiths belonged in the 1850s was rigid and unyielding. Today, however, the Society of Friends is one of the most liberal of all Christian denominations, and is also known for its strong social conscience.

years before, she had become the bride of Dr. James Thomas, a medical doctor and an even more fervent Friend than his brother-in-law, William Nicholson. Hannah's brother, James, at 24, was an earnest and somewhat rigid young man who would surely deplore her defection from the ranks.

"I have thought about this night and day," Hannah went on, plaintively. "The thought of causing such dreadful suffering to my family—" Her voice broke. "I have been asking my heavenly Father if He cannot let me die instead."[2]

Robert patted her hand, quite unable to enter into his wife's sorrow. His own family was only marginal in their attendance at Meeting and in their belief. Robert was emotional and impulsive, but he lacked the deep, steadfast feelings Hannah so painfully expressed.

Hannah set her chin in a look of firm resolution that became so characteristic of her. "I love my family. But my Lord must come first," she stated. "We must do it."

All through the spring and summer of 1859, Hannah agonized over this step. Finally, in September, Hannah took the plunge. First she resigned her right of membership in the Society of Friends. Almost immediately, she was baptized by immersion in the Baptist Church at Pottsville, Pennsylvania, by a German Reform minister. That very same evening, returning to the city, she celebrated her first Holy Communion in Philadelphia at a revival tent meeting, with five thousand other Christians.

Hannah felt a great peace come over her after taking these decisive steps. Perhaps this was a sign of blessing. Hadn't the Whitall family accepted Hannah's spiritual discoveries with love and patience, listening politely to her enthusiastic outbursts? Hannah's father was a warm, good-natured man and described by Hannah as "the best playmate we children ever had." Her mother was "delightful . . . not so full of fun perhaps as our father, but always ready to champion her children's cause at all times; an unfailing refuge to us in every emergency."

Loving and understanding as they were, John and Mary Whitall were unbending in one area. They believed so deeply in their Quaker religion as the true faith that they called it "Truth with a capital T." Quakerism was the whole truth and could not be improved upon.

Little wonder, then, that Hannah nervously twisted a linen handkerchief into a knot as Robert drove her and little Frank in the carriage to the Filbert Street home of her parents one day late in October. John Whitall greeted them at the door—but his usual smile was gone, and his lips formed a grim line. "Thee must come in, since thee is here," he said stiffly, motioning them inside.

Hannah glanced at Robert, whose face remained impassive. John Whitall knew what they had come for. This was going to be more awkward than she'd feared.

Apprehensively, Robert, Hannah, and Frank followed the forbidding figure of her father into the parlor. Hannah and Robert sat down on two straight-backed chairs, and Hannah pulled little Frank onto her lap. Distractedly, she hugged him close, burying her face in his soft curls.

John Whitall's face softened a bit as he spoke to his grandson. "Frank, run upstairs and see if thee can find Grandma."

Hannah released her hold on the little boy and he trotted off obediently on his errand. When he was gone, the door to the study opened and Hannah's brother, James, came into the room and sat beside their father.

"Thee has been a birthright Friend," Hannah's father said to her directly, all softness gone now. "Thee and thy parents and thy grandparents. How thee could do such a thing, bringing disgrace to thy family, I do not know. But this I do know," he said; his voice rose and reverberated like thunder, "I will not have a renegade daughter in my house." That thunderclap was followed by a storm of angry words. "If thee chooses to turn thy back on thy people—on everyone thee loves—I cannot stop thee."

He brought his hand down with a resounding smack on

the arm of the chair in which he was sitting. "I will not have thee in my house any longer, contaminating my family with thy ungodly doctrines."

Hannah was stunned. Robert said nothing. "But, Father," Hannah pleaded, beginning to weep. "Thee has heard how long and prayerfully Robert and I searched. Thee knows we have read and reread the Scriptures before we came to this decision—that as Christians we must be baptized. We resign from the Society of Friends only because we feel we must. Oh, dear Father, doesn't thee see—on grounds of conscience. . . ?" Her voice trailed off.

John Whitall's face was granite, and James was staring at the floor, unable to look Hannah in the face.

"I see no such thing!" her father shouted. "Thee has humiliated thy family *and* caused a stir among the Friends all over Philadelphia. This family will never be able to live down the mortification of thy action."

James stepped forward now. His voice seemed to drip ice as he spoke to Hannah, "And now, if thee pleases, thee will leave this house. Neither here, nor in the house of thy brother-in-law, William Nicholson, nor in the house of thy brother-in-law, Dr. James Thomas, is thee welcome. Remember, it is *thee* who has ostracized thyself from thy loved ones by thy lamentable behavior."[3]

Hannah's face was drained of all color, as she struggled to her feet. Robert, still silent in the tense atmosphere of the room, took her arm and helped her to the door. Outside, she climbed woodenly into the carriage and sat there numb and disbelieving. In a moment, the front door opened again and little Frank ran out to join them.

As they drove away, the clomp, clomp, clomp of the horse's hooves beat like a hammer in Hannah's head.

For all she knew, her family would never speak to her again. She was to them a heretic and a disgrace.

———

Being banned from her entire family was a devastating

blow that Hannah had not expected, but she did not fall apart. In a secret letter that she was able to smuggle to her sister Sally, she spoke of feeling "like an outcast from my earthly father's house. But not, oh thanks be to God, not from my heavenly Father's house! And I know that He is caring for me."[4]

Hannah's decision at the age of 27 to take the radical step of resigning from the Society of Friends in order to be baptized and to receive Holy Communion was an unusual and courageous move. Despite her formal resignation she would hold on to many of her Quaker beliefs, and would even refer to herself as a Quaker later on in her life. Nonetheless, her willingness to accept the fury of her family was evidence of a new steadfastness within and the conviction she brought to her faith.

This decision was also a foreshadowing of her future. More and more, Hannah would find herself clinging to God alone, struggling to depend more on His mercy and love. Soon He would be the only pillar on which she could safely lean.

4

Streetcar Incident

It was a warm spring afternoon in the early 1860s. The windows were open in the Pearsall Smiths' parlor, and the clear sun shone in on the bare, polished planks of the floor. A group of several men and women were clustered around a study table, seated in straight chairs, deep in a discussion about the Word of God. The exchange of ideas was becoming heated, and Hannah, now a matron approaching her thirtieth birthday, was holding firm in her earnest manner.

"I do *not* see," she insisted, her face flushed with feeling, "how a good and loving God could condemn some sinners to eternal torment—while others, no more deserving, should receive the great blessing of salvation." And the feelings of the injustice of it all welled up within her. There were tears in her eyes.

"Mrs. Pearsall Smith," a teacher of the Plymouth Brethren answered sternly, "it says right here in Scripture—in Romans 8, verses 29 and 30, to be exact—that God has set apart and called certain people to receive the good news of the gospel. Everyone is not thus called. We must accept what we read in the Holy Scriptures."

"Forgive me for monopolizing the discussion," Hannah began again, "but this policy of saving only certain people seems inconsistent with the message of forgiveness that I so gladly received in my heart only a few years ago. The God I discovered with so much rapture in the summer of 1858 could not be so disappointing as to cast off a large portion of the creatures He has made with no thought for their final well-being."[1]

Another lady, also a member of the fellowship of the Plymouth Brethren, whom Hannah had joined after her baptism, was becoming uncomfortable. Clearly, she was very disturbed at Hannah's line of reasoning. "Dear Mrs. Pearsall Smith," she said sharply, "we are merely the creatures, not the Creator. It ill behooves us to interfere with the workings of the Almighty."

Here it was—not the first and certainly not the last of Hannah's head-on collisions with those who held, in various ways, to the doctrine of "predestination." To these Christians, belief in God's sovereignty meant seeing God as a righteous judge more than as a loving father. Hannah felt that there was something wrong with the idea that some people were chosen for salvation, while others seemingly were destined for eternal damnation. Predestination seemed to show too little concern for the lost souls as far as Hannah was concerned. She was confused as the meeting came to an impasse. It was a stalemate of reasonings— if not feelings—for the air had become quite charged with emotion. The leader, with a nervous cough, suggested it might be best to close the session with prayer. After this, the various ladies and gentlemen retreated to their separate homes.

Hannah returned to her corner of the sunny parlor, feeling anything but bright in spirit. She was alone now, and the house was quiet. Robert would not be home from work for some time. Frank was still in school. Unresolved doubts churned away in Hannah's mind: One theological issue had troubled her since childhood. How could she know that this same issue had fired bitter disagreements among theologians for hundreds of years? She knelt by her chair, feeling heavy with distress.

"Oh, God," she implored, "how canst thou bear the misery that is caused by sin in this world? In face after face I see unveiled before me, in the marketplace and everywhere, the terrible weight of the suffering and misery that has been brought into the world by sin. It beats upon my spirit like the incessant battering of the waves upon the shore. Oh, God, let me know somehow how thou standest to look upon the face of the earth and behold such awful sorrow. Oh, Christ, I see in thy face a terrible pity over the sufferings of thy fellow human beings."

The turmoil was too much. She *must* know. "Oh, God, I cannot bear it," she prayed, beating her fists on the parlor chair at which she knelt. "Please—*please* give me some ray of light, some illumination."[2]

Tears continued streaming down her face when she rose some time later. But there was no more time for quiet prayer. She had a class to teach that afternoon at the Southern House of Industry, several miles across Philadelphia. Upstairs, she put on her black hat—the one she had specially devised with a heavy veil to cover her face. Hannah had taken to wearing this veil whenever she went out into the street because the sight of every strange face stirred in her such painful reflections on the lot of unrepentant sinners. As she hurried out of her house to catch the tramcar, she felt protected by the veil.

As she was riding the tram along Market Street, however, two men climbed aboard and sat down opposite her. When the conductor came for his fare, she was obliged to raise her veil to count out the coins. And as she did so, she saw clearly the faces of the two men. A flood of anguish took her. The faces, once handsome, were worn down by time and heavy with cares—and besides the slow ravages of time on the face of humanity, Hannah imagined these faces lost in hellish fire forever, if these men were without Christ.

Hannah clenched her hands and cried out in her soul, *Oh, God, how canst thou bear it? I do not see how thou canst . . . endure it.* In this manner, she upbraided God, and felt justified in doing so.*

When her turmoil was spent, though, an inner voice seemed to reply, in tones of infinite love and tenderness, *It is not my will that any should perish but that all should come to eternal life.*[3]

To Hannah there came an awareness that there is to be a final restitution—that is, a making right of all that is wrong. That in the life to come, somehow all sinners shall come to the point where "every knee shall bow and every tongue confess that Jesus Christ is Lord, to the glory of God the Father" (Philippians 2:10–11).

The how and why of it all she could not see, but this one assurance was all she needed—that somewhere and somehow God was going to bring into the fold all the creatures He had created.

It was a rare moment of inner illumination for Hannah. She did not have many in her life, but the ones that came would overturn everything. And whereas the Quakers counted on receiving special guidance quite apart from the Scripture, it became a constant pattern for Hannah that when a shaft of spiritual illumination came her way, it fell *on* the Scripture, breathing life into it. As Hannah would later write, of mystical revelations—by which she meant those that did not involve Scripture: "For most of us, our trouble is that we have the wrong idea of what knowing God is all about—or at least the kind of knowing I mean.

---

*Author's note: Hannah's extreme reaction to human sin and suffering may seem a bit bizarre. Most people don't go outside concealed by a heavy veil in order to avoid the sight of the everyday misery in the world. Ordinarily, Hannah was an emotionally stable person and she was not prone to peculiar behavior. However, her emotions were strained to the limit at this point in her life by the spiritual crisis she was facing. She could not reconcile her experience of God as a God of love with what she was hearing from the church—that God would consign unrepentant sinners to eternal hellfire. How could a merciful God do such a thing? Hannah's feeings at this time were over-sensitized by her own spiritual crisis.

For I don't mean any mystical, interior revelations of any kind. Such revelations are wonderful, when you can have them—but they are not always at our command, and they are often shaky and uncertain. . . . Inward revelations we cannot call to ourselves whenever we will, but anyone in possession of his senses can believe the thing that is written [in the Word of God]. . . . This kind of knowing brings us convictions. . . ."[4]

When she stepped off the tramcar, Hannah was a revitalized person. All through the class at the Southern House of Industry, Hannah's mind was in such a bright ferment that she could hardly wait to end her class and hurry home.

Her feet flew up the steps of the house on Tenth Street. She must check out this wonderful discovery in the Bible to see if it had been there all the time and she had not seen it. And so she sat in her favorite nook in the parlor, Bible and concordance spread out in front of her. The whole book seemed to be illumined. For an hour she read passage after passage of Scripture. Then she closed her books and sat back in her chair, flooded with joy with the new peace that filled her.

Meanwhile, Robert had returned from work, and he and young Frank were talking in another room. The dinner hour was approaching.

Oblivious to all this, Hannah meditated on the new insights that were falling into place, like the simple stones in a spiritual footpath leading straight into the kingdom of righteousness and peace and joy she had longed for for years: God was not a selfish God, visiting His love only on some of His creatures; He was love in its very essence. Love was the very law of His being. She began to think that if her mother heart could love her own children whether they were bad or good, then God must have something like a mother's love too—only infinitely more vast and superior to her own.[5]

She also saw that God's love was not just available for a few of His creatures, as was taught by most religious doctrines in her time, but that the sinners she had met in the street and in the tramcar were also God's precious children. She could not help but think that He loved them all, and she felt reassured that somehow He would see to it that not even the most hardened and depraved sinner would be lost forever.

It was not long afterward that Robert, always lavish with hospitality, was entertaining a celebrated preacher from Boston in their home. The Smiths, in fact, entertained a continuous procession of people with a wide range of religious ideas. On this particular morning, Hannah and Robert were seated at the breakfast table with the Boston clergyman when, with great gusto, the visiting minister started a discourse on the love of God.

"Of course God loves us," he intoned. "But there are limits to what His love can endure. Take mother love, for instance." And he pointed his spoon at Robert. "There are certain sins that a daughter can commit which her mother can never forgive."

Heedless of the scalp-prickling looks that were coming from Hannah, the man went right on. "Yes, there are some sins which are so heinous that if a daughter committed them, the mother would forever close her heart and her home to the child." Then he concluded triumphantly, "And so it is with God. His love goes only so far. And certainly anyone who believes that God will put up with continual sinning holds a senile view of religion."

To Robert's horror, Hannah rose to her feet, her face as white as a sheet, her eyes blazing. Her voice barely under control, she said, "I realize that you are my guest. But the honor of God seems more important to me than ordinary rules of politeness. I will not sit at a table with anyone who so maligns mothers and, even worse, maligns the God who made mothers! Your views of God are intolerable to me. How can you live with yourself as a minister of the gospel and have such an un-Christian idea of the love of God?

"As a mother, I will never cease to love my children, no

matter what they do. God—our loving God—has a heart of mother-love infinitely greater than mine. He never withholds His love from any sinner, no matter how blackhearted or unrepentant the person may be. His love is completely unconditional. Oh, it is too much. I cannot bear to hear a preacher of the gospel say such limited and untruthful things about the love of God."[6]

And here, Hannah lost control and burst into tears. Covering her face, she ran from the dining room.

Robert and the celebrated preacher sat in stunned silence, listening to the sound of Hannah's footsteps as she ran upstairs to her bedroom and slammed the door.

5

Difficulties and Defeats

Though Hannah remained an outcast from her family for some time because of leaving the Quaker Meeting, her sisters continued to be secret allies. They had always been very close, and during the time of greatest family distress, Mary and Sally stood loyally behind Hannah, even though she was able to communicate with them only by letter for some time: Her staunchly Quaker brothers-in-law refused to welcome her into their homes.

Gradually, however, Sally and Mary softened up their stubborn husbands. After some months of cold silence had elapsed, Hannah was once more admitted to their homes. In spite of the vehement opposition of Hannah's father to her defection from the Quakers, he had loved her too long and too dearly to be able to freeze her out of his life for long. By the early 1860s, tempers had cooled, reason had returned, and Hannah found herself once again restored to the bosom of her family.

In the beginning of 1861, however, the Smith family was faced with a new crisis. Robert's publishing business had gone bankrupt because his impulsive nature had led him into many wrong decisions. Pride and a certain degree of arrogance had kept him from confiding in Hannah and others when steps might have been taken to avert this failure. A change of lifestyle was necessary. Their lovely, spacious home must now be rented. Frank's nurse was let go. For the summer, cheap lodgings were found in Atlantic City facing the seashore, while efforts were made to salvage something from the business.

————

Around six o'clock on a particular morning in August, Hannah was sitting on the piazza, hoping the ocean sights and sounds might bring some comfort. She was huddled into a beach chair, with her ever-present journal, inkwell and pen. Heavy, forbidding clouds obscured the sun. The ocean was dark gray and turbulent. Large waves slapped at the cold, wet sand. Hannah pulled her cashmere shawl more closely around her and gave way to her thoughts, which were almost as uneasy as the elements.

I am so afraid that Robert is having some sort of breakdown. He doesn't sleep at night. His thinking is disordered. He takes endless walks up and down the beach, returning all disheveled, with a wild look in his eyes. What will happen to our little family if Robert has a complete breakdown and is unable to work for months, maybe years?

Robert seemed to be at war with himself, which perhaps triggered Hannah's next thoughts about the nation, which was sunk into the depths of the Civil War. *What will be the future of our country if the South wins, as it surely must— the union broken, two separate nations living practically under the same roof? The future looks uncertain and frightening. All around is change and brokenness—in our family and throughout our battle-scarred nation. What will become of us?**

————

*Author's note: As a side note, contemporary readers are often puzzled when reading biographies of men and women of the Civil War era: How could they have lived through such a bloody time in America's history, and seem so little affected by it, at least as the evidence in their letters and journals would indicate? Remember that, in those days, a distance of even fifty miles was

She turned her chair around to the table, and opened her journal and began to write:

Amid many deep and perplexing trials I feel that it is an especial blessing that my faith is not suffered to fail. . . . Though some things which I made special subjects of prayer have seemed to go wrong in every way. . . . The Lord has enabled me to say from the depths of a storm-tossed soul, "Though he slay me, yet will I trust in him." Oh, how I pray that this may continue to be the case. I see trials before me from which my flesh and heart may well shrink unless the Lord shall sustain me.[1]

Hannah closed her journal, straightened her shoulders, and resolutely went inside the boardinghouse. It was nearing seven A.M., and seven-year-old Frank would be waking soon.

The above passage, written when Hannah was 29 years old, revealed the foundation stones of a faith that was to sustain her through even fiercer winds of the soul than those that pounded at her in the summer of 1861. The words "Though he slay me, yet will I trust in him" would come back to her many times in the years that followed.

———

During the winter of 1861–1862, the Smiths lived in a cheap boardinghouse in order to save money. After that, little is known of their fortunes until 1864 when apparently Hannah's father helped them financially. Robert, meanwhile, must have recovered from his partial breakdown. During the latter part of the Civil War, he and his younger

---

vast, and accounts of battles even as great as the bloodbath at Gettysburg came only by wire and newspaper, with nothing at all of the sound and visual impact of the satellite-feeds that penetrate our living rooms today. The war was indeed a matter of endless conversation, and of public prayers in the churches. But for all—especially those with pacifist-determinations, like the Pearsall Smiths, their family and friends—the war was a terrible and *distant* matter. And of course, as is true with each of us, there were still daily pressures of child rearing and making a livelihood. And for Hannah, there was the personally threatening matter of Robert's rising and plunging fortunes, and the darker side of his personality.

brother, Horace, spent some months in a hospital in Harrisburg, Pennsylvania, nursing the wounded. Their Quaker consciences would not allow any of the family to take up arms.

Meanwhile, the Whitall family had bought a large summer home in Haddonfield, New Jersey. They called it "The Cedars." Sometime in May 1864, the Pearsall Smiths were spending a few weeks at The Cedars with Hannah's sister Mary, her husband, plus numerous children.

One afternoon Hannah was sitting in the little back parlor that she had appropriated for herself in the rustic barracks-like structure of The Cedars. A May breeze was blowing the sweet scent of the surrounding evergreens in through an open window. She sat in a wicker rocking chair; at her feet was a cradle. Quietly sleeping there was her three-month-old baby girl, Mary.

After years of barrenness, Hannah had given birth to a daughter who was now filling the empty place left by the death of Nellie seven years before.

Every few moments Hannah bent down to caress the soft cheek and feel the spun-silk curls of little Mary. Even after three months of cherishing this tiny morsel of humanity, her mother still had to touch her many times a day to reassure herself that it was no dream. She expressed some of these feelings in a letter to her sister Sally: *I expected to enjoy my baby—if I should have one, but I never expected such an overflowing gush of love and tenderness constantly welling up in my heart. It sometimes seems awful to have anything so unspeakably precious.*[2]

At that moment the door of the parlor opened and a travel-stained Robert burst in. He had just come from Philadelphia on the train and appeared hot, dusty, and tired. But there was a spark of the old intensity in him as he tossed his silk hat onto the nearest chair and, unbuttoning his frock coat, threw himself down on the wicker chair.

"Well, my dear wife, I have been to see thy father and it is all settled," he announced jubilantly. "We are to move to Millville, New Jersey. I am to be the manager of the Whitall-Tatum Glass Works there."

Hannah was startled. "Thou and father decided it all? Without *one word* to me about all these plans?"

Robert hardly heard her. "With all the debts of the old business, thy father and I have agreed that it was best to make a new start. And just think, dear wife," he said soothingly, "I will be making a good salary in Millville and we shall be able to get back on our feet financially."

"I see," Hannah replied, struggling with her emotions. "Thee and father have doubtless worked out a good plan— but I had not five words conversation in this decision that is to affect my future as well as yours! Of all the husbands I know," she continued, "thee is the only one who treats thy wife as an equal. And now this. I am sorely disappointed."

"I acted in haste," Robert nodded. "But thy father has always advised us soundly. We shall never go wrong if we follow his counsel."[3]

And so, in the summer of 1864, the Pearsall Smiths moved to Millville, New Jersey, a short journey away from Hannah's family. Though Hannah found Millville a dreary, depressing little town, her growing family would keep her busy. Baby Mary was followed in rapid succession by Lloyd Logan, born in 1865. Then came Alice (later spelled Alys) in 1867, and Rachel (Ray) in 1868.

In Millville, too, Hannah discovered a new dimension which enriched her faith. It came about during a period of rebellion and loneliness. She so missed her Christian friends and Bible study groups in Philadelphia that one evening she poured out her feelings to a visiting preacher. He advised her to visit and try to help poor people in her neighborhood.

Hannah obeyed, but soon discovered that the women she talked to suffered from the same spiritual problems she had. "I was like a person trying to feed hungry people out of an empty bowl," she observed. "I went home more discouraged than ever."

Yet Hannah did meet a spiritually alive dressmaker who would occasionally come to the Smith house to sew with her. The dressmaker held the view that there was such a thing as victory over temptation, that it came through a doctrine taught among Methodists, called "The Doctrine of Holiness." Out of this came an experience called "the second blessing," which brought one to a place of victory.

When the dressmaker urged Hannah to come to one of the little meetings they held each Saturday night, where people testified to these experiences, she hesitated. Hannah knew that most of those attending were factory workers. "I didn't think that poor working people had anything to offer me," she admitted. "I had studied and taught the Bible a great deal and felt I had more to teach them than they me."

But one Saturday night Hannah decided to go, filled, as she later put it, "with my importance and superiority." As she took her seat among the ranks at the meeting that evening, a factory woman with a shawl over her head stood up to speak before the group.

"My whole horizon used to be filled with this great big Me," the woman said in the course of her testimony, "but when I got sight of Jesus as my Savior, this great big Me melted down to nothing."

These words penetrated Hannah deeply. *My Me was very big and very self-assertive,* she reported, *and I could not imagine how it could "melt down to nothing." But the conviction came that this was the real Christianity I had been longing for. Needless to say, I did no teaching that night, but sat as a learner at the feet of these humble Christians whose souls had evidently been taught by the Holy Spirit depths of truth of which I understood nothing.*

Hannah began to attend this group regularly. It was here she made the discovery that she had too much depended upon her own efforts, her own resolutions, her own fervency to try to achieve holy living. Now she saw that this was frustrating the grace of God to do a work of sanctification inside her. *I alone can do nothing—and if the Lord*

*does not do it all, it will not be done. But when I trust Him,
He delivers me from the power of sin as well as from its guilt.
I can leave in His care my cares, my temptations, my growth,
my service, my daily life, moment by moment.*[4]

Profoundly influenced by this "Doctrine of Holiness" in
her Saturday night group, Hannah persuaded Robert to
attend the camp meetings held every summer in Manheim,
Pennsylvania, by a Methodist Holiness group. Of special
interest to them was the "second blessing" experience, also
called the baptism of the Holy Spirit. This was to be a
milestone in the spiritual experience of the Pearsall Smiths.

———

One July day in 1868 they arrived at the Manheim
campgrounds, where a big tent was set up for services.
Each family attending brought their own tents and camping equipment. Robert and Hannah pitched their tent under a big tree.

When they awakened the next morning the air was fresh
and clean, birds were chirping. Before breakfast Robert
and a number of other seeking Christians gathered in one
corner of the large tent, all on their knees, praying to receive the baptism of the Holy Spirit. The air seemed
charged with holy excitement. Several who claimed to have
already received this special baptism laid hands on Robert
and prayed earnestly for him to experience this same blessing. After a time of prayer, the little group disbanded.

Robert, deeply stirred by the earnest prayers of the believers, wandered off into the woods to be alone. For some
moments he walked—then, finding a quiet nook under a
large oak tree, he dropped to his knees and continued to
pray. The morning sun warmed him, and all creation
seemed astir with life.

These words were later used to describe what happened: "Suddenly from head to foot, Robert was shaken
with what seemed like a magnetic thrill of heavenly delight
and floods of glory seemed to pour through him, soul and

body, with the inward assurance that this was the longed-for baptism of the Holy Spirit. The whole world seemed transformed to him, every leaf and blade of grass quivered with exquisite color, and heaven seemed to open out before him as a blissful possession. Everything looked beautiful to him, for he seemed to see the divine spirit within each one without regard to their outward seemings."[5]

Robert returned to the main camp as if on wings. There he sought out Hannah as she was fetching buckets of water from the nearby brook, preparing to cook their breakfast. When she saw him coming toward her, his face radiant with joy, she put down her buckets and rejoiced with him in his great blessing.

Hannah, too, longed desperately for this baptism. On the evening of the day that Robert had found this new presence of the Holy Spirit, Hannah was moved by the eloquent testimony of the holiness preacher. Songs of praise resounded through the forest. Seated on her camp stool in the midst of a great throng of worshipers, she prayed fervently. *Let it be tonight, Lord. Let thy servant feel thy power.*

As the preacher invited earnest seekers to come forward, Hannah went eagerly. She knelt by the rough bench that constituted the altar and felt herself on the verge of a wonderful spiritual blessing. She had brought several large handkerchiefs in case she dissolved into floods of spiritual tears. She waited. She felt the Lord's presence—a warmth, a sense that He was near—but no tears came.

All through 1868 and up to June of 1869, Hannah prayed constantly and earnestly for the baptism of the Holy Spirit. She fasted, she sought out the counsel of other spiritual advisors. She experienced no floods of joy, nor any heavenly thrills that shook her from head to toe. Slowly, she became discouraged again about her spiritual state. Something must be wrong with her, she thought, that she was not receiving these blessings.

In June 1869, Hannah and her family were at The Cedars. For once the lodge was deserted except for the Pearsall

Smiths, a Christian friend named James, and another guest, a devout man whom Hannah and Robert had met at the Holiness Camp Meeting the previous summer.

The new family nurse had put the little ones to bed and had retired to her own room. Fifteen-year-old Frank was visiting a cousin. The main room at The Cedars was spacious, with a high-beamed ceiling and an oversized open hearth fireplace. Off in one corner were Robert, James, the visitor, and Hannah, the dim oil lamps casting a half-light on their faces.

Hannah had been fasting and praying for two weeks, almost around the clock. Even in the faint light she looked haggard. With the prolonged loss of sleep, she appeared a little unkempt, and she was extremely tense, jumping at the slightest noise.

James spoke up. "I have spent much of this day meditating on thy problem, dear sister, and it seemed that the Lord spoke to me that the three of us were to continue in prayer and wrestling all night, if need be, that thee will experience the blessed baptism of the Holy Spirit."

Robert nodded vigorously. "I too feel that we must persevere all night in supplication to the Lord on behalf of my wife."

Hannah twisted her hands nervously. "I am determined that tonight is the night. I will pray until I either receive it or fall in a swoon."

All three of them got down on their knees on the bare floor of The Cedars and prayed and prayed and prayed. As the oil lamps grew dimmer, the kneeling figures did not falter. Hour after hour they prayed on. Brother James was exhorting the Lord loudly at three A.M. when Hannah stopped him.

Hesitantly she spoke up, her voice hoarse from hour after hour of pleading. "I think I feel a quiet, weak consciousness of God's presence, like a still small voice. I simply know that the Lord has come in and taken possession of my heart and has set up His kingdom there and that there is nothing more needed, no manifestation of His presence or His love, no melting of heart, no fullness of joy."[6]

In the silence of that darkened room a sweet and holy quiet descended upon the persevering prayers. Wearily, they disbanded and trudged off to bed.

———

Hannah never did experience any emotional evidence to accompany her belief that the Holy Spirit was with her in some fuller, deeper way by faith. She later concluded that what was called "the blessing" was simply the emotional response of emotional natures such as Robert's. To her more practical and rational nature, spiritual truth was imparted as a growing *conviction* about the truth of the gospel—and to Hannah, it was the truth, not the emotions, that set the soul free.[7]

As time went on, she also noticed that emotional experiences very often were not as solid and permanent as the more intellectual ones. Robert, her impulsive husband, had received the baptism in a very dramatic and unmistakable way. Hannah would long for a vivid, tangible expression of God's presence all her life, but never received it. It was ironic that someone with such an erratic nature as Robert's should rise to exalted heights, whereas the steadfast Hannah never had any dramatic manifestations of God's presence.

God was teaching her to trust in Him alone.

6

Crack in the Marriage

In **August** 1872, the Pearsall Smiths were once again vacationing at The Cedars. The golden light of evening filtered in through the windows while a slight breeze rustled the muslin curtains of Frank Smith's bedroom and gently caressed the feverish face of the desperately ill 18-year-old boy.

The breeze was heartening to Hannah, for all day long she had sweltered in the sticky, muggy misery of a typical New Jersey summer heat wave. Frank's bedroom was austere in contrast to the heavily ornamented, carved Victorian furniture of the time. There was a starkness to the plain pine bed, the unrelieved bareness of the unfinished pine walls and the polished hardwood floor.

How like Frank this room is, Hannah thought fondly as she sat on a cushioned wicker chair that she'd brought in from her own bedroom. Her oldest child was such a calm, sedate, good boy, with no unnecessary ornamentation about him either. Ever since his conversion several years before, mother and son had been deeply in tune with each other. Frank took the Christian faith very seriously, and in his first year at Princeton had tried to live in such a way that his life would draw others to Jesus Christ. Hannah secretly rejoiced that he and Anna Shipley, the daughter of her dearest childhood friend, seemed to be falling in love with each other.

Now her dreams for Frank were being threatened by typhoid fever. Once again Hannah was keeping her vigil at the bedside of a sick child.

If only it weren't so hot, Hannah thought as she looked helplessly at the fever-soaked body of her suffering son. It generally took twenty-one days for the fever to run its course and only thirteen had gone by. Could the almost-emaciated body of her eldest child endure the punishment of another week? Frank was so nauseous that it was almost impossible to get any nourishment into him. Hannah moved to Frank's bedside and picked up a cup of beef broth that was ever present on a crude wooden stand.

"Frank dear, could thee swallow even a spoonful?" she asked anxiously. Then she put her arm around his thin shoulders and boosted him up to reach the sustaining liquid. He managed two spoonfuls, then fell back helplessly.

As twilight darkened into night, Hannah lit an oil lamp and sponged his feverish body with a pan of lukewarm water. Toward midnight Frank became delirious. He tossed and turned on the narrow bed, muttering snatches of nonsense. Hannah sat on, watching helplessly from her chair, her lips moving in soundless, fervent prayer. *Thy will be done, oh, Lord, thy will be done, oh, Lord. Thou knowest what is best for my boy. I relinquish him wholly into thy hands. . . .*

All during the night Hannah remained in her chair, praying as the delirium went on and on. Frank thrashed about in his bed, completely out of his head. Toward morning her father entered the sickroom, took one look at the taut, exhausted face of his daughter and laid a hand on her shoulder.

"Hannah, go take some nourishment and get some rest. I will keep thy vigil now." Gently, he pushed his daughter toward the door.

At five o'clock that afternoon the struggles ceased; the

fever-wracked body of Frank lay still. Hannah's oldest child, the boy of whom she was so proud, had gone to be with his heavenly Father.

At first Hannah spiritualized her grief. In her letters she reiterated over and over how unspeakably the Lord had blessed her in taking her darling boy home to be with Him. She insisted that she had always cared more for Frank's happiness than for her own, and if all they believed about the other life was true, then how could she do anything but rejoice when one of her loved ones was taken to its blessedness—to a safe place where his happiness could not be broken?[1]

Two weeks after his death, however, Hannah allowed her true feelings out to Anna Shipley, the daughter of her dear friend. When mother and girlfriend wept together, some of the hurt melted away. Hannah was able to say to the older Anna, "I dare not go into the depths of this sorrow. After a while, when the keen edge is gone, I shall be able, perhaps, to look it more fully in the face and to speak of it."[2]

In 1869, the Pearsall Smith family had left Millville, New Jersey, and moved back to Philadelphia to a house right next to Hannah's father and mother, on Filbert Street. It was there, during the fall of 1872, that Robert began to suffer a serious and complete nervous breakdown.

In those days, the treatment of emotional illness was still quite primitive. If the sufferer had the money, he went to a sanitorium-type place, usually in a resort setting. Thus we find the whole Pearsall Smith family at Clifton Springs, New York, in October of 1872 living in a large rest home run by a man referred to only as Dr. Foster. There were at least five stories in this "curing place," quite likely an old-fashioned hotel with Victorian turrets and cupolas, and surrounded by woods and meadows.

Hannah was miserable at Clifton Springs. She felt cut off from her support group, her parents, sisters, and dear old friends. Her grief over Frank's death was still fresh and painful. This was not the time to be stuck in a large resort home for invalids, among a group of strangers, away from her familiar people and places. To assuage her grief Hannah had started to write a book, her first, about Frank. She titled it *The Record of a Happy Life,* and wanted it to record the story of her "noble and glorious boy," hoping that it might help others who were going through bereavement. To obtain privacy for writing and also to work through her own pain, she hung a sign outside the door of her rooms on the fifth floor of the sanitorium that said, "Busy writing." In early November the manuscript was finished and sent to the Fleming H. Revell Publishing Company.

On December 13, H.W.S. (as she frequently referred to herself) had finished her dinner in the elaborate Clifton Springs dining room. Because Robert was unpredictable in his emotions, she had dined alone, and now she was standing in the large, drafty hall, shivering in spite of her warm woolen dress and heavy shawl. She was waiting for that "new-fangled" invention, the elevator, to take her to their fifth-floor rooms—wondering what she would find. With a clatter, the contraption settled itself at the first floor. Hannah entered the "cage" and pulled back the lever to start the thing on its perilous ascent. The little box vibrated and the cables squealed and finally stopped with a sudden jolt at the top floor. Stepping from it, she reluctantly approached their rooms.

She had left Robert in quite a state of upset. Five-year-old Alice was also in the rooms, though bedridden with a persistent fever, a sore mouth, and no appetite. Since the oversized building could not be heated properly, Hannah herself was exhausted and chilled. Eight-year-old Mary and four-year-old Ray were in another part of the hotel, attending a sewing class. Seven-year-old Logan had run off after dinner to be with a friend.

With her false teeth* chattering slightly, she opened the door to their apartment. Robert was slumped over in a chair. All the color had drained from his face and he was wild-eyed. When he saw his wife enter, he sprang from his chair and began to pace up and down. "Pray for me, Hannah, pray for me," he begged. His usually well-modulated voice came out in a hoarse croak. "Pray for me to be delivered from this unbearable torment." He struck his fist against the frame of the door again and again with resounding thuds. "Oh, God, oh, God. Let me die."

Hannah's own nerves were as raw as flayed flesh, but she lowered herself calmly into a chair and spoke softly. "Will thee try to compose thyself by repeating over and over the Lord's Prayer?"

With the capricious turn of mind of the mentally ill, he turned on her. "Thee doesn't understand me! Thee doesn't understand a nature like mine. Thee is like a slow-moving stream with placid ripples. I am like a roaring mountain brook rushing over rocks, churning into wild cataracts."

Hannah tried to keep her voice calm. "I know I cannot always understand thy ups and downs."

"Thee is so unfeeling!" Robert shouted. "I need love from a wife! I need warmth and touching and tenderness. Thee is like a dry old stick. I'm sure I could get well if only thee could get thy dead emotions kindled."

Struggling to withstand this barrage of accusations, she answered quietly, but with a tremor in her voice: "Thee must take me as I am, Robert, and not try to change me. I accept that thee is a tempestuous, emotional man and I love thee for thyself." Her voice became pleading. "Please, Robert—won't thee *try* to love me as I am? I love thee dearly, and if it were not for the fact that thee has become so constantly dissatisfied with me, I should feel that I had a husband just suited to me."

---

*Author's note: It is not known how Hannah lost her teeth, simply that they were gone by 1872. She had had four babies in the 1860s. In those days, women who had several children in rapid succession often lost their teeth, probably due to a calcium deficiency during pregnancy.

Robert stood threateningly over the smaller, calmer figure of his wife. "Thee doesn't know how thee hurts me. Thy indifference and the things thee says without thinking. Is thy skin as thick as a rhinoceros?"

Hannah defended herself wearily. "I can assure thee that I mean nothing but love and kindness. My whole heart grieves over thy sufferings, and I am longing to do anything I can to alleviate them. I cannot help being the sort of person I am. And if thee could make up thy mind to try to bear with me patiently and to overlook what is displeasing to thee, perhaps thee might be at least comfortable, if not happy."[3]

At this moment sick little Alice, who had been fitfully sleeping in the adjoining room, woke up and began to cry. With a glare at his wife, Robert stormed across the room and exited, slamming the door. Heavy with the weight of all this emotional upheaval, Hannah slowly dragged herself to the bedside of the sick child. Fortunately for Hannah's own sanity, Alice would get well. Her overstrained nerves could hardly have endured another death so soon after Frank's.

It was probably true that Hannah Smith was not a sexually responsive woman. Like most Victorian wives, she was reared to be passive and not to enjoy sex. Most Victorian husbands, in fact, took it for granted that sex was a "duty" to their wives and did not try to make intercourse pleasurable. Too, the main problem in male/female relations a hundred years ago was the overly dominant role every male was trained to assume. Victorian wives often saw sex as another assault, another assertion of male supremacy, and resisted it.

Something else happened at this rest home that upset Hannah. Dr. Foster secretly passed on to select patients a "spiritual" discovery that he had made. He said that in his prayer time alone he had experienced physical thrills that he thought belonged to earthly passions. At first he was embarrassed that such sexual feelings accompanied his spiritual searchings, but he seemed to have one of those incidents of spiritual guidance, apart from the Scriptures, as if God's voice were telling him that the physical feelings were a manifestation of the Holy Spirit.

Hannah was immediately skeptical about Dr. Foster's "revelations," although Robert listened with some interest. For Robert's own sake, he should have ignored the whole thing.

———

Around Christmastime the whole family journeyed by train back to Philadelphia. Robert had calmed down and seemed somewhat better. When his ailment returned in the new year, however, the family and his doctor decided that he should go back to Clifton Springs by himself while Hannah and the children remained behind in Philadelphia. As the relapses continued through February, doctors suggested a trip abroad. A change of scenery was thought to be beneficial for mental trouble.

Thus it was that in March 1873, Robert took the steamer to England with the intention of continuing across Europe to Switzerland to a place called Mannedorf. There thousands of cures for mental illness had been reported. Robert was also instructed that if he did not find help in Mannedorf, he was to take a soothing journey up the Nile River in Egypt, since such a journey was regarded as a panacea for mental ailments in the 1870s.

All the doctors thought that Robert's breakdown was brought on by overwork, and rest was prescribed as a cure—total rest for a period of months. Imagine Hannah's surprise when she heard that soon after Robert had arrived in England, he had thrown himself into the thick of evangelical work there. In the summer of 1873, she reported to her sister that Robert was involved in the Mildmay Conference, holding crowded meetings of two, three, and four hours' length, teaching and exhorting in his peculiarly effective way.[4]

Hannah knew that Robert was in one of his high periods and not taking care of himself. To add to this worry, she was pregnant again at the age of 41—her seventh pregnancy.

———

There was an irrepressible quality in Hannah Whitall Smith that the death of beloved children, the upsetting behavior of her husband, and a pregnancy in her forties could not quench. It came out during the summer of 1873 while the family was in Atlantic City.

One rainy June morning the children were restless. They had been promised a sail, and the weather had not cooperated. Hannah shooed them into their bathing costumes—nine-year-old Mary, seven-year-old Logan, six-year-old Alice, and four-year-old Ray, plus assorted cousins. Clothing her enlarged body with a huge "waterproof" and grabbing an old-fashioned, oversized umbrella, Hannah marched the complaining children outside to the beach.

The rain pelted down as Hannah directed traffic, her feet planted in the wet sand. Looking like a tent with an umbrella over it, she supervised the children, who soon forgot that rain was a bore and began to frolic in the water. Their mother acted as a games coach, calling out instructions and ideas for water tag from her citadel on the beach. Finally, hungry and tired, the drenched but happy group scampered back to their boardinghouse for dry clothes and a big dinner of roast beef.

That afternoon, with the rain still pelting against the windows, Hannah decided to pay a call on her sick mother-in-law, who resided a few blocks away in a rooming house called The Chalfonte. She had armed herself in her rain gear again and was prepared to set out when her mother appeared.

"Where is thee going, daughter?" asked Mary Whitall anxiously.

"To The Chalfonte to see Mother Smith," replied Hannah matter-of-factly.

Mary Whitall stared at her in stricken silence. "Thee has only two more months to go in thy condition. Surely it isn't proper for thee to show thyself in public?"

"Oh, Mother," laughed Hannah, "thee must not take on so. It is, after all, a purely natural event. It cannot be so bad for me to stick my nose out the door."

Mrs. Whitall shook her head skeptically. "It was never done in *my* day. Women in an interesting condition never went outside or mingled socially after the fifth month. It doesn't show proper modesty."

Hannah bent and kissed her mother's cheek. "Thee will see. I will not meet anyone in this rain, and I will pay only a very short visit." With that she was gone, leaving her proper mother staring after her in appalled wonder. Pregnant women—out in the streets? What was the world coming to?[5]

That evening, when things were quiet and the children were in bed, Hannah sat in a quiet, enclosed parlor with her portable writing desk. The new gas lights were lit, casting a bright light that illuminated the whole room. What an improvement they were over the old oil lamps! She looked at them admiringly. It used to be so hard to see at night unless one sat practically on top of an oil lamp.

In the softened glow of the gas lights, Hannah began a letter to Robert. Her handwriting was characteristically neat and legible: *Thy last private letter gave me heartache and some sleepless hours. But I have laid the whole burden off on the Lord, for I am helpless. Thee says it is only friendship that I feel for thee. But I do not understand it. I cannot comprehend any love different from that which I feel, and I do not think I want to . . . and I believe I will not strain myself in seeking after something that I cannot even conceive of. If it is only friendship I feel for thee, darling, it is at least pure and true and . . . finds its happiness in thy happiness.*

I am very sorry for thee that thy wife is the sort of person

*she is, but please, please, do take me as I am, and not insist
upon my being unnatural. I do not feel as if I could endure
any more of the strain of the last two years! I suppose I am a
pragmatic sort of person, incapable of the heights and depths
of love. Well, darling, I did not make myself; and if thee tries
very hard, I think thee might perhaps put up with me, as I am
for the few remaining years of our life.*[6]

Hannah found that her hands were trembling as she
finished the letter. *Will it never end?* she thought. *Over and
over again, the same old arguments, wearing a groove in my
mind, like a merry-go-round with its music off-key, going
round and round, over and over.* She heaved her bulk off the
chair, gathered up her writing materials, and headed for
her bedroom.

Morning dawned, gray and gloomy. Water dripped from
the eaves above Hannah's bedroom window. The beach
looked lonely and desolate. She woke with a start, for her
dreams had been disturbing. She made a move to climb out
of bed, then fell back with a sigh against the pillows. She
had dreamed that Robert came home from England just as
sick as ever—with the same old sleepless nights, wild, tormented thoughts and scenes of accusation that she had
lived through at Clifton Springs the previous autumn. A
wave of despair washed over her; her spirits were as damp
and bedraggled as the incessant rain outside.

"Oh, Lord," she prayed half aloud, "if it be thy will,
spare us this sorrow. But—dear loving Father—I commit
Robert to thee and leave him in thy hands. And I know that
somehow, no matter how things seem, that thou dost do all
things well."[7]

In August, Hannah and family were back at The Cedars
in inland New Jersey, again suffering from a prolonged heat
wave. Hannah was for the most part confined to her room,
waiting daily for the baby to come. She had become quite
depressed from the weight of so many family troubles, also
with the oppressive heat and her advanced state of pregnancy. On August 8, she wrote to her cousin Carrie, always

a close friend and confidante: *Life with its failures has pressed upon me of late with the most unspeakable sadness; and I have felt such an intense sympathy with the Lord Jesus in His sympathy with the sufferings of this poor fallen world.*[8]

In late August a little girl was born—a perfectly formed infant, but stillborn. It was the final setback to a year of defeats and disappointments.

Oh, Carrie, I did long for my baby so inexpressibly, she wrote to her cousin. *No one knows the need I have of just the comfort a baby always brings to me; and I had looked forward to this baby more longingly than ever before. But I know God's will is best; I have literally made the will of God my pillow for the last few weeks . . . and have hushed all questionings and anxieties by repeating over and over and over: "Though thee slay me, yet will I trust thee."*[9]

7

A Time of International Fame

Though Hannah's private life was eroding, her public life was about to flourish. When they had been at the Holiness camp meetings before Robert's breakdown, she and Robert had been introduced to a new doctrine that some theologians call "perfectionism." This was a belief that there were two parts to the life of salvation in Christ. The first part was, of course, to accept the free gift of Jesus' death on the cross for forgiveness of sins and be restored to harmony with God. The second was a further step in faith and involved trusting Jesus to give the believer an increasingly sinless life.

This second step was usually associated with the baptism of the Holy Spirit and meant that Christ "in" the Christian was transforming his or her life, making one more perfect and more able to conquer besetting sins, one after another.

This doctrine was preached as the "higher life," and Robert was expounding it eloquently in England while Hannah was explaining it to smaller groups in Philadelphia and even in Atlantic City. Hannah was beginning to make a name for herself as a Bible teacher and preacher. As more and more people came to hear her, she was obliged to try to find a larger room than any house could furnish. Since churches of her day generally frowned on any sort of spiritual leadership by women, finding that "larger room" was difficult. Finally, Hannah and her supporters did locate a church liberal enough to let her use one of their Sunday school auditoriums.

By the 1870s, Hannah had no church affiliation and was pointedly nonsectarian. She had begun to attend Friend's Meeting again and apparently was welcomed back to the fold with no hard feelings.

Her book about Frank, *The Record of a Happy Life,* had become a bestseller and was translated into several languages. She had frequent disagreements with Robert by mail about the English edition. Apparently the publishers had omitted the "thees" and "thous" that the Quakers always used in everyday speech, and had substituted "you." Hannah was very upset about this and strongly urged that the "thees" and "thous" be restored.

Robert's preaching ministry in England continued to grow. When he urged Hannah to join him in Great Britain, she and the children sailed for England early in 1874.

To her unspeakable joy, she discovered that Robert's nervousness was entirely gone. United in a mutual dedication to the Lord's work, there was less friction. Robert had rented a furnished house at Stoke Newingham in London. Hannah had barely settled her little family there when she was invited to a luncheon party that was set up to introduce her to the British evangelical world.

Now, Hannah was well aware that some of her teachings were of concern to some of the clergymen of her time. She had raised questions about the many sinners who failed to come to the saving knowledge of Christ because of ignorance or because of horrible, degrading life circumstances. Her conviction was that God's love for His children is so overwhelming He would find a way to restore lost sinners to His presence. This was the doctrine of "restitution," which she had adopted some time before. Though a number of religious groups today espouse this viewpoint, in Hannah's time such a belief was much in the minority. Practically all the clergy preached hellfire and damnation.

Hannah's message was basically this: God is the Creator of every human being; therefore, He is the Father of each one and they are all His children. Furthermore, Christ died for everyone, and is declared to be the "propitiation" not for our sins only but also for the sins of the whole world (1 John 2:2). However great the ignorance or grievous the sin, the promise of salvation is without limitation, whether it happens in this world or the next.[1]

Hannah believed that people needed a vision of the God of love, mercy, and tenderness, and she pointed to numerous New Testament passages showing that mercy was central to its nature.

And so she went to this London luncheon knowing that an inspection committee of British evangelicals was coming to see if the wild woman from America was presentable. She was determined to be on her best behavior.

So Hannah, now 42, sat in the parlor of her hostess' house, dressed in respectable black, her still-blond hair discreetly covered by a small lace cap. The maid had set platters of sandwiches on tables scattered throughout the room. The ladies perched stiffly on the uncomfortable chairs that were fashionable in Victorian times, their cumbersome taffeta and silk skirts gathered around them. Gentlemen in frock coats and mutton-chop whiskers removed their tall hats and settled themselves on horsehair sofas and chairs.

To Hannah the atmosphere seemed strained and unnatural. The British made polite conversation in a very stilted manner as they stole frequent looks at their guest from America. Hannah smiled to herself—perhaps these very formal English people expected her to gulp her tea from her saucer or commit some other unpardonable breach of social etiquette. A sudden thought came: *These people are all sitting here with long faces. They need something to cheer them up.*

So she said in a lively manner, "I've just seen a funeral. I do like funerals."

The august assembly politely tried not to gape at Hannah. They lowered their eyes, nervously studying their teacups.

Hannah went on brightly. "And I always give thanks when I see the casket. I'm thankful that the brother or sister has been delivered from the trials and pains of this mortal state."[2]

One of the evangelical ladies was staring fixedly at Hannah now. She was Georgina Cowper-Temple—later, Lady Mount Temple—an influential and wealthy member of the British aristocracy whose husband owned a stately home named Broadlands, in Hampshire. She was so fascinated by what the strange American was saying that she forgot to be circumspect. She blurted out, "Is it possible? Do you give thanks for everybody's deliverance?" There was an inaudible gasp among the ladies and gentlemen present.

I've done it, thought Hannah. *The men have been in such a fuss over my restitution views. And here I've gone and put my foot in my mouth first thing. But now that it's out in the open, I have to tell the truth.* She swallowed carefully and answered, "Yes, I do. For I believe in the goodness of God."

The company of British evangelicals sat as if rooted in their chairs. There was a moment of horrified silence. The very air of the room seemed to crackle and vibrate with tension. It was Mrs. Cowper-Temple who broke the ice. She rose to her feet, adjusted her gown, swished across the room, and planted a kiss on Hannah's cheek. Then she faced the whole room. "I'm going to have a conference at Broadlands, and you, Mrs. Smith, must come to talk of this."[3]

And so, in July 1874, Hannah and Robert went to the beautiful estate of Broadlands at the invitation of Mr. and Mrs. Cowper-Temple to hold the first of three conferences that were to have a lasting effect in the British religious world. About two hundred people attended. Some fifty guests stayed in the mansion itself; undergraduates camped out in the park-like grounds of the estate, while the rest rented rooms in nearby villages. During the six-day conference, Hannah's preaching was as much admired as Robert's.

The meeting at Broadlands was such a success that Robert decided to organize another one, "The Higher Life," at Oxford. This conference was held from August 29 to September 7, 1874. It was attended by some eight hundred to one thousand people and was a resounding success. There was also great interest in the special series of ladies meetings conducted by Hannah. When the six Pearsall Smiths boarded the steamship *Ohio* in late September to return to the United States, they did so with a feeling of deep fulfillment.

Most people would have collapsed on board ship after such an exhausting expenditure of spiritual energy. Not Hannah. Although she was usually seasick during voyages, such was not the case this time. She invited other passengers to a meeting in the steerage section. She was somewhat hampered by the fact that she had lost her false teeth during the course of the Oxford Conference. If her usual precise diction was slurred a bit, though, she compensated with extra enthusiasm.

Not all of her listeners were sympathetic. Some of the crew, fortified by shots of rum, had come out of curiosity. When challenged to give up their sinful lives, the members of the crew responded with jeers and catcalls. Hannah stared at the men firmly and went right on with her message. Suddenly there was a swishing noise through the air and a greasy wet dishcloth landed right on her face. Hannah paused, took a clean handkerchief from her reticule, carefully wiped her face, and continued as if nothing had happened.[4]

During the following winter the Smiths settled down to a normal routine until Robert sailed for Europe on a preaching tour in early March of 1875. Hannah, meanwhile, divided her time between her children and her newly launched career as a writer and speaker.

From her journals and letters, it was obvious that she was often a fun mother. One stormy morning, for example, Hannah was just coming down the stairs after nursing her eight-year-old Alice through a fever, headache, and diarrhea. Logan, now nine, was standing at the bottom of the stairs brandishing a long coil of rope. He was going through a stage of fascination with ropes and pulleys and learning to tie different kinds of knots.

"Look, Mother, what I found in my wardrobe," he announced happily, swinging the rope. "Remember when I used to tie you up before we went to England? Will you sit down in that big chair and let me see if I can still do it?"

Hannah very seldom turned down a request that would add to the enjoyment of her four darlings. Smiling wryly at the thought of household chores that would have to wait, she sat down in the big chair. Logan was ecstatic. He uncoiled his rope and skillfully trussed his mother up in the chair.

The bell pull rang and Logan ran off to answer the door. Mother Whitall came in. Possibly she was startled to find her daughter roped tightly to a large chair, more likely not. Little that Hannah did surprised her anymore.[5] Reluctantly, Logan untied his mother and ran off to play.

Hannah had an unusual capacity to switch quickly from one passionate concern—like restitutionism—to another, like temperance. During this period, Mother Whitall and Hannah were together often in what they considered the great movement of the age—the crusade against alcohol. Victorian women saw drunkenness as the chief cause of poverty, child abuse, and crime. Their current project was to persuade all the Whitall clan to sign the pledge, a card passed out by the Women's Christian Temperance Union in which the signer swore to be a teetotaler.

"I'm a pretty good mush spoon," Hannah often said of herself. By this she meant she could stir things up. Soon she was stirring up her brother and his family with an eloquent temperance speech, after which she smilingly presented them with pen and pledge card.

James and his wife, Mary, were visiting his parents when Hannah arrived with speech and pledge book. They signed and their daughter Saidee did the same. By now Hannah was convinced she needed to get all her friends and acquaintances signed up and could hardly wait until she joined Robert in England to shove the pledge book under his nose.[6]

Meanwhile, Hannah remained a controversial person overseas. Robert had written that Mr. Blackwood, who was his primary religious backer in England, had expressed some doubts about whether Hannah should be part of the Brighton Conference in the summer of 1875. In the first place, she was a woman preacher and this was unheard of. If that wasn't enough, there were her views on "restitution." A committee was meeting to decide Hannah's fate.

With tongue in cheek, Hannah picked up her pen and began a letter to Robert: *I quite enjoy the thought of thy powwow over me and of Blackwood's condolences with thee on the possession of such a dangerous article as a heretical preaching wife. . . . Give my love to Blackwood and tell him what an irrepressible case I am. . . .[7] Tell him also that I do not care to be "endorsed" by anybody. And as I have not the least desire to preach unless the Lord wants me to, He shall be my only backer.[8]*

By now Robert was an international figure, mesmerizing large audiences with his preaching. He had been invited to Berlin, where Kaiser Wilhelm I had placed at his disposal the old Garrison Church. Robert made a deep impression on thousands of souls in German cities which was attributed to the power of the Holy Spirit, especially since he could speak no German and had to have an interpreter. He took as his battle cry a single sentence from a German hymn: "*Jesus erretet mich jetzt* (Jesus saves me now!)."

The response to his preaching was almost hysterical. When engraved portraits of him were put on sale, eight thousand were sold in a week. The news of Robert's vastly successful work in Germany reached Philadelphia by telegraph. The newspapers reported it like this:

> *Berlin, April 16. The success of the revival mission of Mr. Robert Pearsall Smith in this city and other towns in Germany is increasing.*
> *Immense crowds attend the meetings and members of the nobility occupy seats on the platforms. The Empress Augusta has given a private audience to Mr. Smith.*[9]

According to Logan, Robert was reported to have said exultingly, "All Europe is at my feet."

When Mr. Blackwood had finally cleared Hannah for the Brighton Conference, the first thing she did was go to the dentist and have a spare set of false teeth made. She had no intention of being caught without teeth in case she lost them as she had the year before. In spite of Robert's phenomenal success, however, Hannah was not looking forward to the hectic schedule of religious conferences and meetings that had been set up. When she and the children finally boarded the steamship *Pennsylvania* in late May, she wrote to her sister: *I cannot tell thee how dreary the show-life I have to live this summer looks to me in prospect. I feel just as if I were a sort of traveling Barnum's Hippodrome* (circus) *with a "woman preacher" on show instead of a tightrope dancer.*[10]

Hannah was miserably seasick most of the trip. She lay on her bunk in the stateroom as the steamer *Pennsylvania* pitched and tossed in the rough seas of the North Atlantic. Her head throbbed, and every time she tried to get off the bunk her stomach turned flip-flops. Finally she made a heroic effort to rouse herself. There was work to be done. Her stomach heaved as she struggled gingerly to her feet and lurched across the stateroom to her desk. There before her was a partly finished manuscript. She lowered herself onto the desk chair and tried to focus her eyes on chapter 20. It was titled "The Life on Wings" and was the last chapter of a book that had been nothing but drudgery from start to finish.

The story behind *The Christian's Secret of a Happy Life*—the book she was trying to complete—is intriguing. In 1873, Robert had started a little paper called *The Christian's Pathway to Power*. When he became involved with his preaching ministry, he had trouble producing material for the paper and so prevailed upon Hannah to write an article for it. She reluctantly agreed to write one article if Robert would stop his daily drink of wine that his doctor had prescribed. As she put it, "The article was dragged from me at the point of the bayonet."

Robert was somewhat nettled to discover that his wife's first article excited more interest than anything else in the paper. There was nothing for him to do but put pressure on her to write another and another and another. She claimed she did not feel any sense of being called to write them, beyond the fact that she wanted to oblige Robert. In fact, she described herself as feeling most uninspired. A publisher asked Hannah to put the articles in book form, and she had promised to finish the last chapter before she arrived in England.[11]

The Christian's Secret of a Happy Life, published in 1875, has sold millions of copies and is hailed as a religious classic. The phenomenal success of this particular book, out of all her writings, led Hannah to say that "to do things from a sense of duty is as likely a road to success as to have a feeling of inspiration." She often used her seasickness as the text for a plain and pointed moral lesson: Feelings were unreliable; faithfulness was the important thing. Whether she felt inspired or uninspired was beside the point. It was God who did the work.[12]

———

When the *Pennsylvania* docked in England, Hannah had to get the children settled at Monkhams, the Essex estate belonging to her wealthy Quaker friend, Mrs. Henry Ford Barclay. Then she was rushed off to Brighton to a conference of some eight thousand people gathered from all parts of the civilized world. Hannah gave two duplicate Bible readings, one at three in the afternoon and another in an adjacent room at four. Between two and three thousand people attended each of these Bible readings, and she had to shout to make herself heard in the immense room. Since all this was before the era of loudspeakers, Hannah became, as she said, "as hoarse as a crow."

The poor German pastors present found themselves in a dreadful predicament. They were firmly convinced that it was wrong for a woman to preach, yet they were eager to hear the controversial American. They announced they were attending the conference under protest, swore they wanted no part in such scandalous goings-on, and yet would sneak in each day to hear Hannah, hoping that no one would notice.[13]

Robert had reached his finest hour, preaching to thousands, stirring many hearts with his emotional messages. While his outpourings moved many to tears, Hannah handled her teaching in a plain, vigorous manner. There were even people who complained that she made her listeners laugh during her meetings.

These meetings had a lasting impact in the British evangelical world. The Keswick movement, which continues on to the present day, had its beginnings in the Brighton Conference of 1875.

Only one small episode marred this triumphal time for the Pearsall Smiths. After one of the meetings an adoring fan of Robert's rushed up to him, threw her arms around his neck, and kissed him.

Hannah later asked her husband who the woman was. "A Miss Hattie Hamilton," he replied.

"I thought she overstepped the bounds of good taste," Hannah commented.

Robert shrugged it off. "I am like a father to her. Don't take it seriously."

Far better for Robert if he had.

8

Robert's Fall

Exhausted when the Brighton Conference was over, Hannah decided to go to Switzerland for a rest. She left England on June 14, with 11-year-old Mary and her cousin, William Hilles, for a two-week trip through the Alps.

She negotiated the Channel crossing on her return trip without being sick, and was seated in the train in Dover waiting for it to depart. She was on her way back to Monk-hams to visit the children and to meet Robert so that they might continue on to the many conferences that had been arranged for them for the rest of the summer.

Hannah rested her head against the green plush seat of the train and wondered why it was taking so long for it to get moving. She was feeling very thankful and satisfied about the last two years. The Lord had poured out so many blessings. Robert's nervousness was entirely gone. He had become a world-famous preacher. There was sweet accord once again between husband and wife as they did the Lord's work together. They were comfortable financially at last, and back in America her latest book was already in popular demand in the bookshops. On the home front, they had four intelligent children. Hannah was just thinking about her eldest daughter, Mary, who was growing into a beautiful and poised young lady. She took special delight in this child. . . .

At that moment a telegraph boy came running down the platform, shouting, "Telegram for Mrs. Pearsall Smith."

Hannah waved at him through the open window.

The telegram was from Mr. Barclay and read: *Mr. Smith ill in Paris at the Hotel Louvre. We think you should return to him at once. All conferences given up.*

Hannah was deeply disturbed—and perplexed. Robert had no preaching mission in Paris; he was supposed to be in England at the Keswick Conference. A quick change in plans was made. Mary went on to the Barclays with the other adults in their party, while Hannah returned alone by the night boat to Paris.[1]

As she traveled through the darkness, fidgeting uncomfortably in the ship's lounge, Hannah's thoughts churned. What could have happened? Her last news of Robert had been so different. Why had Robert fled from England to Paris? Was it another breakdown? Over and over, she had to force her troubled thoughts to turn from doubt and fear to the soothing refrain of one of the Brighton hymns: *"Trusting as the moments fly, trusting as the days go by; trusting Him whate'er befall, trusting Jesus, that is all."*[2]

When Hannah arrived at the Hotel Louvre, she longed for nothing more than a hot bath and sleep. Her eyes felt gritty from being awake so long, but she straightened herself resolutely and marched up the stairs to her husband's room.

Robert was prostrate on his bed, too ill to eat or sleep— a wild, tormented look on his face. Hannah recognized, with a sinking heart, the same old symptoms of nervous disorder. He looked as he did during those nightmarish months when he was at the sanitorium at Clifton Springs, in the fall of 1873.

"Robert, why is thee here?" Hannah spoke gently.

Robert could only talk in jerks and fits, a phrase or two at a time. "I left London . . . wanted to come on to Switzerland to be with thee." His voice was a dry, cracked whisper. "Couldn't get that far . . . too sick. Collapsed here."

Hannah folded her hands together and tried to ignore the fact that they were trembling. "But, dearest husband, why? Why is thee not at the Keswick Conference?"

Tears came unbidden to his eyes and rolled down his face. "Mr. Blackwood," he began again, "told me I must not preach. . . . Canceled all meetings."

"Darling," she answered, altogether puzzled, "what made him do such a thing?"

At this, Robert roused himself from his semi-stupor. His voice came out clearer than before. "Does thee remember Miss Hattie Hamilton?"

"Yes," replied Hannah, "I remember her being very free with thee at Brighton—thee told me that thee thought of her in a fatherly way."

"I did think of her in a fatherly way," Robert said bitterly. "But there was more. After thee left for Switzerland, she requested a private interview with me. It was late at night and she asked me to come into her bedroom. I thought at the time that that was not quite proper, but her spiritual distress seemed so great." Here Robert stopped and groaned.

Hannah was feeling tense, but managed to keep her voice quiet and even. "And what happened then?"

"Well, Miss Hattie was crying in a very uncontrolled way. She seemed almost in hysterics. She was sitting on her bed shaking all over and telling me over and over that she didn't feel that Jesus had accepted her as His child. She looked so forlorn there, so lonely and sad. I went over and sat beside her on the bed and put my arm around her to soothe her." Robert's voice faded away.

"I did not feel attracted to her," he protested after a moment. "I only felt toward her as a father might feel toward his child who needed comfort. And, as the two of us sat together on the bed, I explained to her the precious doctrine that Dr. Foster told us about at Clifton Springs. I told her how Christ wanted us to feel thrills up and down our bodies because this would make us feel closer to Him."

"No!" Hannah gasped. She leaned her head back against the chair for a moment. "Thee *didn't* tell her that! How many times have I warned thee of passing that doctrine in secret to thy female followers? I told thee before that that was a delusion and could only lead to trouble. Why did thee not give heed to my warnings?"

Robert held his hands to his head. "Oh, my head aches so. I can't bear to think about this anymore. Please, let me try to sleep."

"Yes," Hannah went on patiently. "We must call a doctor and he will give thee drops to help thee sleep. But first, I must know the rest. What did thy 'fatherly comforting' have to do with Mr. Blackwood?"

Robert groaned. "Miss Hamilton went to Mr. Blackwood the following morning and told him that I had explained to her the physical thrills that a man and a woman can experience together while holding each other and praying. That is *not* what I told her," Robert said vehemently. "And she said I had tried to make love to her. That is not true."

"But Mr. Blackwood is thy friend and sponsor"—Hannah was aghast—"he will not believe that conniving little liar."

"Oh, but he did. He did believe her." Robert kneaded Hannah's hand with his nervous fingers. "He never even consulted with me. And he called all the other ministers in for a meeting and told them all that she had said." Robert was on the verge of breaking down again. "He believed her, and the other ministers believed him. I didn't even have a chance to defend myself. The next day he called me into his office and informed me that all the meetings were canceled. I was asked to cease all preaching."

Robert released her hand and rocked back and forth. "I sat in Mr. Blackwood's office and started to cry. I was angry with myself for losing my dignity like that, but I couldn't help it. I lost control and I sat there and cried. I told him over and over that I had nothing but a fatherly feeling for Miss Hattie, that I was sorry for telling her about the secret doctrine. Mr. Blackwood did not believe me."[3]

Robert's escapade with Hattie Hamilton was eagerly reported by the press. The *Brighton Weekly* headlined it: *Famous Evangelist Found in Bedroom of Adoring Female Follower.* With that kind of publicity, Robert's preaching career in Europe was destroyed.

Hannah stayed on in the Hotel Louvre for several days with the trembling, frightened shell that her husband had become. When reason seemed to return to the broken man, she persuaded him that the family should return to America. Later she wrote to a friend: *Robert has had a complete breakdown. He has lost twenty pounds already and is suffering very much from almost constant nausea. But the Lord has taught us the lesson of living by the moment, and I am not anxious.*[4]

And so the Smiths left the scene of their widely publicized religious triumphs and returned in disgrace to America.

Weeks later, to silence the British newspapers, which had gleefully pounced on Robert's "scandal," the Brighton Conference Committee released the following statement:

> *Some weeks after the Brighton Conference it came to our knowledge that the individual referred to (meaning Robert Pearsall Smith) had, on some occasions, in personal conversation, inculcated doctrines which were most unscriptural and dangerous. We also found that there had been conduct which, although we were convinced that it was free of all evil intention, was yet such as to render action necessary on our part. We therefore requested him to abstain at once from all public work, and when the circumstances were represented to him in their true light, he entirely acquiesced in the propriety of this course.*[5]

The Smiths settled uneasily in Philadelphia at the Filbert Street home, which was next door to Hannah's father and mother. Since her father was becoming quite feeble, she spent most of her time caring for him, Robert, and her children, finding very little time left for public work in the year that elapsed after the Brighton disaster. Robert went sluggishly to work and tried to enter into the family doings—but the heart had gone out of him.

Hannah wrote to her British friend Mrs. Barclay in June 1876:

> *It makes my heart ache to look at my dear husband and think of the blight that has fallen on him. You think that I make a mistake to say that his life is blasted. You would not say this if you knew him. A more sensitive, tender-hearted, generous man never lived, and this blow has sorely crushed him in every tender spot. He often says to me that his life is one long agony. . . . It could not be otherwise, and I have not the faintest hope that he will ever recover from it. There are storms which uproot and overturn even the stateliest of trees and what wonder then if the weaker ones are utterly prostrated by them? My life is full of the dear children's interests and of the sweet cares for my husband and parents. A commonplace life is, I am sure, the most desirable for a woman.[6]*

But Hannah was not destined to lead the commonplace life for very long. Robert's religious colleagues and supporters in the United States were determined to reinstate him in the eyes of the religious world. Neither Robert nor Hannah had any desire to go back to the life of preaching or teaching; but after repeated entreaties, the Smith husband-and-wife team agreed to appear at the Framingham Conference in the summer of 1876.

And so in July, Robert and Hannah dragged themselves away from the quiet restfulness of The Cedars and arrived with reluctance in Framingham. By the fourth night of the conference, Robert was preaching with all his old fervor. His voice rang out over the convention hall urging the congregation to holiness. Sinners wept. There was an overall consciousness of the presence of the Holy Spirit. As Robert spoke, those present felt the touch of God's power in their lives. When he finished his sermon with an altar call, many came forward.

Back inside the hotel bedroom, Hannah lit the gas lights as Robert collapsed on a chair. "What a wearisome performance," he moaned. "I am counting the hours until we can get away and go back to the seclusion of The Cedars."

Hannah stared at him in surprise. "I don't understand it, dear husband. Although I cannot imagine a meeting begun in a worse frame of mind, yet blessings were pouring out."

"There is no enthusiasm in my heart," muttered the exhausted Robert. "The meetings are a bore. The work is a treadmill. I don't know how I can hold out for two more days."

Hannah was thoughtful. "Then the hand of the Lord must be truly at work. He was there both in my Bible lessons and in thy preaching."

"Well, let the hand of the Lord do it then," Robert replied petulantly. "I just want to get out of here."

Hannah shook her head in bewilderment. "They all say this is the best meeting ever held in this country. And it really is a good meeting. I can sense here the same wave of blessing as swept over our English meetings. It so upsets all my preconceived notions that I do not know what to make of it."

Robert sighed wearily. "As for me, no matter how much they beg, I am done. No more meetings. Someone else may preach."

"No matter how confused we feel about the meeting," Hannah concluded, "it is a satisfaction to see thee treated with all the old deference and respect. No one even seems to remember the English scandals."

Robert stayed to the end of the Framingham Conference, but by 1877, he was having increasing doubts about his beliefs. In fact, he was in the process of losing his faith altogether. Hannah's internal conflicts were of a different nature. Her logical mind had trouble making sense of the events of the last two years.

Robert's disgrace at Brighton had been a terrible blow. Two years later, Hannah was still trying to understand why the Lord had allowed it to happen. She and Robert had certainly been doing a fruitful work for the Lord. Then—why?

Carefully she went back over the section she had written about this in *The Christian's Secret of a Happy Life*:

The life of faith becomes an impossible and visionary theory if we believe that human beings can come in and cause trouble for us and that God does nothing about it. What good is there in trusting our affairs to God if, after all, man is to be allowed to come in and disarrange them? And how is it possible to live by faith if human agencies, in which it would be wrong and foolish to trust, are to have a prevailing influence in molding our lives? . . . To the children of God, everything comes from their Father's hand, no matter who or what may have been the second causes or agents to bring it about.[7]

Hannah had therefore concluded that "God is in everything" that happens to people who have committed their lives to Him.

Because Hannah believed that for the Christian, God directs the events of his or her life, she was forced to assume that the Brighton episode had come upon them direct from the hand of God. Blackwood and his friends may have been the actual instruments that brought about Robert's embarrassing dismissal from the Lord's service, but God must have allowed it to happen: indeed, must have wanted it to happen for some reason.

This line of reasoning upset Hannah very much and tried her faith to the utmost. Why would God want this to happen? What was wrong with her and Robert that God wanted them to cease their active labors for Him? Why didn't God stop Blackwood from jumping to conclusions and believing Miss Hattie Hamilton rather than Robert?

To add to Hannah's state of confusion, there was the question of the baptism of the Holy Spirit. During 1876 and 1877, she had again sought diligently for this blessing since numerous Christians among her friends and acquaintances were receiving floods of blessings from the experience. Yet, as she put it, "I remain a dry old stick."

Hannah could not help but wonder why Robert was granted the blessing so richly and then seemingly had allowed it to slip away when she longed and yearned in the fiercest kind of way to receive it and never "felt" anything.

Questions about God continued to plague her. For two years—from 1876 to 1878—her letters expressed her anxiety and doubt. Since faith in God was the most important thing in Hannah's life, her anguish of spirit must have been beyond belief as she feared that she was losing it.

On June 5, 1877, she wrote to Robert, who was traveling extensively on family business matters, that the unbelief of her heart was terrible.[8]

June 20 she again wrote pathetically to Robert: *I want thee to promise not to whisper a word of thy perplexities into my ears. It is a ticklish seat on top of a greased pole and the least push one way or other might upset me.*[9] She felt her spiritual flabbiness to be such a danger that she went out of her way to make an effort to surround herself with Spirit-filled Christians so that she might maintain her precarious hold on her faith. She admonished Robert to do the same— to surround himself with mature believers: *I think it is a very critical time with thee, and if thee wants to get back to the old place, thee must put thyself under the right sort of influences.*[10]

She was to have been one of the leaders of a religious convention in 1877. This seemed, to her, preposterous, and she told a friend, *I don't know how I can do my share at that meeting unless my soul is satisfied first.*[11] She felt like a "pygmy" among baptized women, and went through a period of feeling that she had failed to receive the longed-for baptism because of her unbelief. She spoke of herself when she said, "The teacher of faith finds herself needing to be taught the very first principles."[12]

By May of 1878, Hannah was still going through a severe testing time, spiritually. Robert was now taking almost a hostile attitude toward matters of faith. But Hannah was made of sterner stuff. Like the house built upon a rock, she stood firm against the storm. Writing to her friend Anna Shipley on May 20, she said:

By faith I claim that I have the baptism of the Spirit. And it really does seem to me that if the Bible is true, I must have it. But I am just the same as ever, and find no change whatever in my inward experience; and therefore I feel sure there must be something wrong. Perhaps it is not knowing the inward voice. But one thing I know, and that is that I am all the Lord's and that His will is infinitely and unspeakably sweet to me. It grows lovelier all the time, and I wonder how anyone can fear it or rebel against it. And like a poor little child who has lost its way, I creep into the dear arms of my Father and just ask Him to carry me, since I cannot understand His directions. He doeth all things well and I can leave myself with Him.[13]

9
Adventurous Hannah

Hannah Whitall Smith's resiliency would surprise people all through her life. Knocked down time after time, hounded by doubts and confusion, she had a gift for dealing with defeat and rebounding from despair. There was a prevailing buoyancy in her soul, an aliveness and sense of adventure in her spirit.

Hannah would have said very simply that her constantly deepening faith kept her from losing her enthusiasm for life, that it was her steadfast belief in the goodness of God that lightened her spirits and enabled her to maintain her vitality.

And there was something else that kept springing up out of her personality like a jumping jack. Hannah had a pungent sense of humor that was often directed at herself. This came out in the accounts she left of her travels, especially camping trips.

One such excursion took place in July 1878, in the Adirondack Mountains in upstate New York. Hannah, then 46, entered into the plans with such gusto, her children were sure that the whole idea was most appealing to her.

The Pearsall Smith party was camped at the edge of a beautiful mountain lake. On this day the rain was coming down steadily. The tent leaked. Mother Hannah sat on a camp stool under the driest section of the soggy canvas and hoped that her clothes would be protected by the tarp she had wrapped them in. A high hissing whine sounded in her ear. Another mosquito was poking for blood on her hand. She slapped at the mosquito and put away the circular letter she was trying to write to her relatives and friends.

Smoke poured into the tent through the partially open flap. Hannah coughed and tried to wave it away. Outside, her niece and nephew, Carey and Tom Thomas, were valiantly trying to keep a fire going in the persistent drizzle. The smoke from the fire was supposed to discourage mosquitos, but this species seemed to thrive on it. Meanwhile the guides, hired to direct the Pearsall Smiths on their trek through the Adirondacks, had managed to prepare a rabbit stew over a little stove under a grove of big trees.

Hannah called to her children, who were rowing happily on the lake. They returned to shore, drenched but cheerful, and they huddled together at a birch-log table. Everyone tried to keep the rain from dripping into the stew. Hannah had covered herself with a waterproof and tried to enjoy the wild grandeur of the mountains and the serene loveliness of the lake, but it was no use. The dampness was in her bones. Her stew was soggy! Mosquitos continued to dive-bomb her. She was miserable.[1]

The next day the rain had stopped and the guide led them through the primeval woods and virgin forest. The party had to cross several little streams that had single log bridges. Hannah tried, slipping and sliding across them and, at length, just marched through the ankle-deep water, rather than trying to negotiate the log bridges. She went on ahead of the rest of the party and followed the trail by herself for a long time.

At last she sat down on a log to wait for the others. She waited and waited. No one came. All she could hear was the uncanny stillness of the primeval forest and the faint rustlings of wild things in the bushes. It wasn't long until she began to imagine that some of the rustlings were bears. Her overactive imagination conjured up a dreadful scene with a huge bear rising out of the mysterious depths of the woods, tearing her limb from limb and making a feast of her until nothing was left but her skeleton. When the rest of the party finally arrived and found only the bones of their beloved relative, they would form a circle and weep piteously until someone put her pitiful remains in a casket for burial.

The real Hannah was still sitting on the log, waiting for the others to catch up with her. Whatever was in the bushes seemed to want to stay there. However, she frightened herself so with her imaginings that she got up and fairly ran back along the trail until she encountered her nephew Tom Thomas and one of the guides.[2]

The truth of it was that Hannah detested camping, but since the children loved these trips, each year she endured with cheerful fortitude the hard beds, incessant rain, persistent insects, and the aching muscles of middle-age.

———

Three summers later, still avoiding public life, the Smiths explored the area around what is now Yellowstone Park in Wyoming. Four guides and nine family members needed saddle horses, a large mountain wagon, three baggage wagons with tents, provisions, stove, etc., and finally, a dog named Buster, whose function it was to guard the camp. This impressive cavalcade wended its way along the rough roads of the natural, unspoiled wilderness near Yellowstone in the warm months of 1881.

Hannah got along fairly well as long as she was able to ride in the big mountain wagon and didn't have to sleep in the open air. At Tower Creek, however, the rocky trail was too narrow for the mountain wagon. Hannah had to select a horse to ride. One of the guides produced a sober old creature named Foxy.

Hannah studied Foxy with wary eyes. Foxy stared back

boldly, as if assuring her that he had carried a pack for years and was too mellow and experienced to do anything foolish or frisky. Hannah patted him on the neck gingerly and managed to heave her bulk into the saddle. She and Foxy took their place at the end of the procession as they all set out for Yellowstone Falls.

The trail led through mountainous country. In the high altitude the sun shone brightly. Picturesque rocks jutted out from the hillside. The air was balmy and sweetly scented with pine. Hannah began to relax and hum a quiet little song to herself.

All of a sudden Foxy, who had fallen behind the rest of the horses, became upset. He began a series of strange maneuvers—he backed up and went forward and went to the side and turned round and round and neighed indignantly. Then he gave an unexpected jump. Poor Hannah sailed over his back and landed on the ground under his feet in an ignominious heap.

She was not hurt. Early on, Hannah learned how to relax while falling. Foxy, however, was apparently greatly chagrined by his bad manners. He stood still, twisted his head around, and eyed her in a contrite way while she struggled to her feet.

Hannah could have yelled for help. Instead, the undefeatable Hannah brushed herself off and painfully hoisted herself back up onto Foxy.[3]

———

In August 1883, Hannah, then 51, found herself dragged off to Maine for yet another camping trip. Robert, claiming illness, remained at home. The Pearsall Smith children, assorted cousins, and the reluctant chaperon, Mother Hannah, arrived by stage at Moosehead Lake, where they hired a steam-propelled yacht to take them around the lake.

August 11 found them at the mouth of the Kennebec River. The yacht was tied to the shore and Hannah and family spent a relaxed day canoeing, swimming, and picking berries. The children came dashing by carrying light canoes.

"Where art thou going?" murmured Hannah. The peaceful lapping of the water against the rocks had been lulling her to sleep.

"Mother," answered Logan, "we are going to carry these canoes upriver and ride the rapids back."

Hannah had developed rheumatism, and her joints ached constantly. She was overweight. Nevertheless, with an adventurous gleam in her eye, she hoisted her complaining body to its feet and announced decidedly, "Well, I am coming too. I have always wanted to shoot the rapids."

A bit later the four canoes were lowered into the water, with Hannah enthroned in state on several life preservers in the middle of the first canoe. Logan was in the stern and Mary in the bow. Someone pushed the canoe into the middle of the swirling, foaming water, and it whizzed on through the white water, bounding along, veering from side to side, a thrilling and hair-raising ride. The mother sat majestically, her eyes sparkling with delight. At the end she said calmly, "Well, that was fun. Let's do it again."[4]

During this trip the guides took the Smith family to a logging camp, which meant a four-mile walk through the primeval forest over a rough logging road. Hannah valiantly plodded along with the others. She had on her cast-off clothes, which were spattered with mud. On her feet she wore huge clodhopper boots, encrusted with grime. An old blue felt hat was jammed down over her untidy hair; several damp strands hung down in her face. There was a mud splotch on her cheek. She was a bedraggled and forlorn-looking figure as she pushed herself on with her walking stick.

The Smith family was nearing the end of the hike. The others were ahead of poor Hannah. She looked up, wiping her dirty hand across her face, smearing the mud. Coming toward her on the trail were several dapper-looking gentlemen, fresh and spruce, just starting out on their walk. With consternation, Hannah recognized Professors Phelps and Farnam of Yale and Reverend Newman Smythe, author of *Old Faiths in a New Light,* a book on Christian evolution, which Hannah had read and with which she had been much impressed. In fact, she had written Mr. Smythe a letter asking him a knotty theological question about Adam and Eve. It was too good an opportunity to be missed.

Hannah intercepted Professor Phelps and his party and introduced herself. The three men stood, rooted to the spot, and stared at the disheveled-looking lady whose limp, sweat-soaked hair was hanging down in her face. Professor Phelps, with a fastidious hand, brushed an imaginary speck of lint off the sleeve of his immaculate jacket.

"Reverend Smythe," intrepid Hannah spoke up boldly, "I wrote thee a letter some time ago asking thee why God forbade Adam and Eve from coming to the knowledge of good and evil. It seemed to me a necessary step in their development, and that I should have thought God would have wanted them to come to this knowledge. They would have been mere animals otherwise."

The reverend was dumbfounded. He was not prepared for this formidable woman, who had materialized out of the wilderness and was asking him difficult theological questions. One did not expect to go for a walk in the Maine woods and all of a sudden get plunged into a thorny debate about original sin. He stared at his mud-spattered opponent and tried to marshall his thoughts.

"Ah, um," he stuttered. "Well, ah."

"Yes?" prompted Hannah relentlessly.

"I, ah, have your letter in my trunk at Mount Kineo and was meaning to answer it this summer," he stumbled on. Poor Reverend Smythe closed his eyes, thinking perhaps that this whole episode was a figment of his imagination.

"I would so much like to hear your views on this subject," she continued undaunted.

"Well, yes." He was beginning to collect himself. "I was thinking about your question and feel sure that I will have something to say about it soon. Actually," he hedged, "no one has ever spoken to me on this subject before. Although," he finished magnanimously, "I have often wondered why they have not."

"Well, I will let you know if I have any light on the subject," offered Hannah, trying to be helpful.

"Yes, yes, thank you. And I will write you as soon as I have considered this matter thoroughly."

Hannah bowed politely and stepped aside to let the three gentlemen pass. They continued on down the trail, shaking their heads in a state of amused bewilderment. One never knew what one might meet up with while traipsing around in the wilds of Maine.[5]

It was not only in the United States that Hannah's children insisted on her sharing their adventures. When Logan became greatly enthused about culture on the European continent, nothing would do but that his mother must enjoy it too. He and his cousin Harry Thomas dragged her to art galleries all over France, Germany, and Italy. But, like a faulty vaccination, none of this exposure to the old masters "took." Hannah could not like the great paintings of Europe no matter how hard she tried. She decided that there was something wrong either with her or with the artists. But she had a basic inner curiosity to go anywhere, to try anything.

So it was that Hannah found herself trudging up endless European mountains to see lonely ruins at the top, searching out strange religions to find out what they offered. She visited Turkey and rode in a sedan chair lined with yellow silk, which she said made her feel like a harem woman. Once she met a gentleman from North Africa who owned a ruined Greek temple and was anxious to sell it. With great difficulty, Hannah restrained herself from buying it.

She admitted to having purchased a little lake in Florida with eighty acres around it because she wanted to own the alligator who lived in the lake. She had also acquired some land in Wyoming for the sake of owning property in a state where women had the right to vote. As time passed, Hannah seemed barely to slow down. In a circular letter to friends, she wrote that she had within her a creature that was possessed with an unquenchable longing to do and to see everything there was to be done and seen.

It is a most uncomfortable creature to have within one, she went on to say. *For after hearing some new thing, it is never satisfied until it has had an experience of that thing. I sometimes wish nobody would ever tell me of anything new, for of course, if I do not hear of new things, this inside creature will not hunger after them.*[6]

It was obvious that the adventuresome side of Hannah had not greatly changed from the irrepressible teenager who defied Quaker preaching to view the naked statue of Leander in the Philadelphia Academy of Fine Arts.

Hannah—a "dry old stick"? Hardly.

10

When Does a Woman Know?

In June 1877, Hannah's father died. He had been paralyzed for some months before his death and failed very rapidly through the winter. As Hannah recorded it: *He fell asleep in Jesus, just like a tired child falling asleep in its mother's arms. It was a sweet, peaceful, close to a noble, completed life.*[1] Rather than dwell on her loss, Hannah rejoiced that her father was "safely gathered," her quaint term for the departed loved one who is released from the sufferings of this life.

Life went on in the Smith family. In the summer of 1878, they were all at The Cedars with assorted cousins. Mary was then 14, Logan 12, Alice 11, and Ray 9. Robert had returned from his second trip to the west coast, having put on so much weight he could barely get into his clothes.

On a warm July evening Hannah was preparing for bed after an exhausting day helping the children to construct a lawn tennis game. She lowered her tired body into the rustic but seemingly sturdy bed in the austere pine-walled bedroom that had been Frank's room until he died. She yawned and sighed contentedly. The bed felt good to her aching muscles. She had left the oil lamp burning for Robert (gas lights had not yet come to the woods of New Jersey).

Soon she could hear him stomping up the stairs. He entered the room and, with much grunting and assorted noises, removed his clothes and boots. Hannah was drifting off to sleep when he heaved his corpulent body onto the bed. The much-abused bed groaned under his weight; then, as he thrashed about, trying to get comfortable, there was an ominous splintering crack. Hannah found herself doubled up in the mattress as it sagged to the floor.[2]

In a sad way, this broken marriage bed was symbolic of the deteriorating relationship between Robert and Hannah.

In the fall of 1878, Mary was sent to Howland College in New York. This "college" would be regarded now as a private high school. In the 1870s, however, there were very few schools for girls that offered twelve grades of good instruction. The Smiths had to send Mary hundreds of miles from home to provide her a quality education. Hannah was determined that her daughters should have the college education that she herself had wanted so desperately and had been unable to receive. Mary, an intelligent girl with a thirst for knowledge, went along enthusiastically with her mother's plans.

Logan, 12, suffered from attacks of malaria. Through family connections he was able to spend the summer of 1878 in the rarified climate of Wyoming where he recovered his health. That fall, Logan and Alice, now age 11, went to a boarding school in Providence, Rhode Island. Ten-year-old Ray, the most spiritually sensitive of the four, the daughter closest to Hannah in thought and style, remained at home.

Early in 1880, Hannah's mother passed away peacefully after a short bout of pneumonia. Hannah missed her mother very much but always rejoiced in the deaths of elderly people, and considered her "safely gathered."

In the latter part of January, Alice and Logan were sent home from the Providence school. There had been an epidemic of scarlet fever at the school and both children had light cases. The children were delighted to receive an extra holiday, and the house on Filbert Street resounded to the cries of children dashing in from afternoons spent skating on a nearby pond or sledding.

Then Ray took sick with scarlet fever. This terrifying, nineteenth-century child-killer had gotten a severe grip on Ray. For three days her body burned with fever as Hannah hovered at her bedside. Helplessly she watched the relentless disease sap away the life of her precious youngest child.

On February 7, Hannah's forty-eighth birthday, she was lying in bed beside her fever-baked little daughter. Tenderly she sang a hymn to soothe the sick girl. Twilight was seeping into the room even though it was not yet five o'clock. All of a sudden the watchful mother observed that Ray was no longer breathing. The child's face was radiant with a surprised, happy smile, as though she had seen a glorious sight while passing from life to death.

It was well that Hannah was granted this blessed sense of her youngest child's happiness in heaven, for she herself ached with pain over the loss of the one child, of all her children, whose spirit was closest to hers. Ray was, as Hannah said in a letter to Anna Shipley, *a most uncommonly mature little thing. . . .*[3]

Hannah's last entry in her journal—begun thirty-two years before, in 1848—was dated December 30, 1880. In it she summed up her feelings about the death of Ray: *Since I last wrote in this book, my mother and my darling little Ray have both gone home to God. My dear mother was feeble and aged, and though her going left a great blank, yet we could not but feel thankful to have her spared any further weariness or sorrow in this world. But little Ray, our youngest, our perfect little girl, was only 11, and her life was full of promise. For her loss there was no comfort, but simply and only the sweet will of God. As I sorrowed, I began at once to say, "Thy will be done," and that blessed will has surrounded me like a fortress from that moment to this and I have been able to say to myself:*[4]

"Meanwhile," the mother cried, "Content!"
Our love was well divided;
Its sweetness following where she went,
Its anguish stayed where I did.
Well done of God to half the lot,
And give her all the sweetness.
To us the empty room and cot,
To her the heaven's completeness.[5]

Elizabeth Barrett Browning

Losing four of seven children by death would make any mother question God's goodness, even in an age when child deaths were frequent. How ironic that the author of the bestseller *The Christian's Secret of a Happy Life* should have her faith so put on trial! Hannah's pious letters to her friends, rejoicing in the "safe gathering" of her children, seemed to reach out for an understanding she didn't quite possess. Having warned her readers not to trust feelings on matters of faith, she was determined not to buckle under the tidal wave of personal blows dealt her in the years that followed. She dug in for a continuing assault, by the enemy—and it came.

In one area, however, the Smiths had no problems. There was continuing financial prosperity, thanks to the Whitall-Tatum Glass Works and to the able management of John Whitall. After his death, Hannah and Robert received a considerable income from the family business. Shortly after the death of Ray, the Smiths moved from their house on Filbert Street to a much more spacious dwelling at 4653 Germantown Avenue. The children had horses in Germantown; Robert had a pony phaeton. Hannah, a good household manager, was able to hire sufficient domestic help to relieve her of many of the housekeeping chores.

By the end of summer 1880, events must have occurred to destroy the blind trust Hannah had in her husband's moral integrity. Some of these might have taken place on a family trip to California that summer when Robert planned to introduce his wife and children to friends he had made on previous trips. For some reason she refused to meet his friends. It was a low time for Hannah anyway as she was still mourning for Ray and she was also going through menopause. She told her sister afterward, "Somehow it did not seem worthwhile to go on living any longer."[6]

What had happened? No letters or journals pin down the exact experience that caused the final rift in Hannah and Robert's marriage, but from later statements by family members and other circumstantial evidence, it is possible to assume that something like the following scene took place:

Early in January 1882, Hannah set aside a day for sorting clothes. Nonusable items were given away. It was a yearly ritual. She cleaned out Alice's and Logan's wardrobes and moved on to Robert's rows of suits hanging tidily in his big old upright mahogany chest.

The cuffs of one coat were badly frayed. It was one of his favorites, but was now distinctly scruffy. Hannah took it down from the hanger and was going through the pockets, preparing to throw it out. There was a crackle of paper in the inside pocket, and Hannah drew out a crumpled letter. Ordinarily she would have ignored such a letter, but there was something about these crumpled sheets that stabbed her heart. Two sentences caught her eye as she stood there, holding the offending papers gingerly in her hand.

"Come and see me when you can, darling. I am always ready to entertain my sweet Robert."

She read the words before she could stop herself. A slow flush suffused her face. She sank down in Robert's big leather-covered armchair, her heart pounding, unable now to stop reading the letter.

The love letter left no doubt in the mind of his wife that the "female friend" was more than a friend to Robert. The big house on Germantown Avenue seemed suddenly very quiet. Not the slightest noise penetrated to the lonely reaches of Robert's third-floor bedroom as his stricken wife sat limply in the chair, her flaccid hand dangling over the arm, still absently holding the repulsive letter. She leaned her head back against the fragrant leather and memories flooded over her.

She recalled the romantic walks along the beach in the moonlight during their courtship thirty-one years before. She remembered the first days of their housekeeping together and how proud she had been of her handsome husband. Later memories came: Robert holding her in his arms as she sobbed out her grief after Nellie's death in 1857 . . . the sense of togetherness they had felt at the camp meetings at Manheim, Pennsylvania, in the 1860s . . . Robert hugging her tightly after he had received the baptism of the Holy Spirit during his morning walk in the woods . . . the sense of exaltation when Robert's mellow, persuasive voice rang out in the halls of the Oxford and Brighton conferences . . . the many times after praying together when the sense of the Holy Spirit had filled the room.

Where had it begun to go wrong? Brighton—in 1875? That public humiliation had soured him.

Hannah had to admit to herself at long last what she had refused to face before: Robert was weak. . . . *Please, dear husband,* she could remember writing to him, *I wish thee could bow thy neck submissively to the yoke the Lord has put upon thee and not question His dealings. It would take the sting out of thy troubles at once.*[7]

She believed that Robert should have stood firm in the integrity of his purpose, confessing his mistakes, but refusing to reject any truth of God because of these mistakes. She believed that if he had done this, God would have sustained him. But Robert had let the unsanctified part of himself get the upper hand. As his faith drained away, his vitality had left too. His charismatic personality faded and now he was becoming a self-indulgent old hypochondriac, irresponsibly investing their money in foolish speculations.

Hannah's sadness gave way to indignation. She remembered the terrible strain of the months of Robert's nervous breakdowns, the sleepless nights during which she had maintained a staunch loyalty to her spouse. And this was how he had repaid her. She crumpled up the letter that was still in her hand and threw it violently to the floor.

And so Hannah went through that fateful day in January 1882 with a lead weight in her heart. Mechanically she did her chores and thanked God that all the children were away at school. When Robert came home for the evening meal, he was so self-absorbed that he did not seem to notice her stiffly formal replies to his comments. She said nothing about the letter, for she had burned it in the stove. Thus the rift between husband and wife widened.

After dinner when Robert had left the house for an unknown destination, Hannah headed for her favorite corner at the end of the parlor where her special writing table and chair had been set up. She longed to sob out her grief, but crying would not help. Instead, she went through her pile of unanswered letters until she found the one that had recently come from her friend Priscilla Mounsey, who lived in England. A lovely spinster lady, Priscilla had written of her depression and loneliness. This now touched a responsive chord in Hannah. Getting out paper, pen, and inkwell, she began to write:

> *The loneliness thou speaks of I know all about. For do not think, darling, that it is confined to unmarried people. It is just as real in lives that have plenty of human ties: husbands and children and friends. . . . And I believe [God] very rarely allows any human love to be satisfying, just that this loneliness may drive us to himself. I have noticed that where a human love is satisfying, something always comes in to spoil it. Either there is death, or there is separation, or there is change of feeling on one side or the other, or something, and the heart is driven out of its human resting place. . . .*

Now, darling, thy loneliness is not only because thou art unmarried and has no very close human ties. It is the loneliness of a heart made for God, but which has not yet reached its full satisfaction in Him. Human love might for a while satisfy thee, but it would not last. If thou can only see this and settle down to it, it will help thee very much. Thou wilt give up, as I have, any expectation of finding satisfaction in the human creature, and will no longer suffer with disappointment at not finding it. And this will deliver thee from the worst part of the suffering of loneliness. Thee will accept it as a God-given blessing meant only to drive thee to himself. . . .

Thy circumstances are lonely, but thy loneliness of spirit does not come from these; it is the loneliness of humanity. Therefore, nothing but God can satisfy it. No change of circumstances, no coming in of the dearest earthly ties . . . could really satisfy for any length of time the hungry depths of thy soul. I am speaking, darling, out of the depths of my own experience when I say this, and thee may believe me.

But now the question is how to bring oneself to be satisfied in God when there is no feeling. And I do not know what else to say, but that it must be by faith. . . . I confess that it does seem an odd sort of thing to do, to become satisfied by saying one is satisfied when one is not. But is it not just what faith is described to be, "calling those things which be not as though they were"? What else can we do?

In my own case, I just determined I would be satisfied with God alone. I gave up seeking after any feeling of satisfaction. I said, "Lord, thou art enough for me, just thyself, without any of thy gifts or thy blessings. I have thee and I am content. I will be content. I choose to be content. I am content." I said this by faith. I still have to say it by faith often. I have to do so this very evening, for I am not very well and feel what I expect thou would call "low." But it makes no difference how I feel. He is just the same, and He is with me, and I am His, and I am satisfied. . . . [8]

Hannah Whitall Smith, 1886, in the midst of personal tragedy and public acclaim.

Robert Pearsall Smith in 1875, a year of evangelistic fervor and scandal.

Hannah with her first-born, Nellie, c. 1852. Bronchitis would claim Nellie's life on Christmas Day, 1857, at age five.

Ray (seated), Logan, and Alys, 1874. A bright summer of adventure in England.

Mary, 1874. Pretty and brooding.

The Whitall women: Mary, Hannah, and Alys, 1898.

Mary, 1880.

1885—Mary's husband,
Frank Costelloe, whom she
would abandon with their
children, ages two and four.

1909—The artist Bernhard
Berenson who offered Mary
a life of "freedom" in Italy.

Charming and intellectual, the outspoken atheist Bertrand Russell swept Alys off her feet in 1894. Unfortunately, he was as strong in his convictions as Alys was weak in her faith. The match was devastating.

C. 1883. At the height of her public life, Hannah spoke out, not only on matters of faith, but frequently addressed groups from the women's Christian Temperance Union and was a leader in the campaign for women's suffrage.

At Friday's Hill, 1894. Standing: Alys and Logan. Seated L-R: Robert, granddaughter Karin, Hannah, granddaughter Ray, and Mary. Beneath the calm surface the tensions were palpable. Mary was estranged from Frank Costelloe, father of Ray and Karin. Alys was being courted by Bertrand Russell. Robert was now an outsider to the faith, pursuing clandestine relationships.

Hannah and Robert enjoy a word game at Friday's Hill in 1894, several years before Robert was "safely gathered."

11

Battle for Women's Rights

Hannah Whitall Smith was knocked down by a relentless series of blows in her latter years, but she was never down for long. There was a resilient quality in this pioneer of women's rights in the nineteenth century. Although motherhood was always her number one commitment, she found time to go to temperance meetings, to preach, teach, and speak on all kinds of social issues.

Deeply upset about the position of wives in Victorian society, she joined with Susan B. Anthony and Elizabeth Cady Stanton (famous early advocates of women's rights) and gave stirring speeches advocating women's suffrage, appalled that women were not considered responsible enough adults to vote.

She believed intensely that if women had the right to develop their minds, liberation would follow. "Girls should be made to go to college at bayonet point," she once remarked. Hannah advocated everything short of blackmail to force the consent of reluctant fathers of nineteenth-century women, who usually considered higher education for their daughters to be not only superfluous but a downright drawback to their marriage potential. What husband would want to be "saddled" with an educated wife?

Her most successful convert was her niece, Martha Carey Thomas, the eldest daughter of her sister Mary and Dr. James Carey Thomas. "Minnie," as Hannah called Carey, was very close to her aunt as she was growing up, and showed considerable intelligence at an early age. By the time she was 17, she was determined to go to college.

Carey's father, more liberal than most Victorian men, was still aghast that a daughter of his wanted to ruin her life by pursuing an advanced course of study. In 1874, no reputable young lady would even think of destroying her chances for a good marriage by becoming educated. Members of his family sympathized with him in his refusal to consent to a university for Carey. Dr. Thomas remonstrated with Carey. He told her he didn't have the money to send her to college and was already overburdened with the support of eight children.

There must have been something in the Whitall family that encouraged independence of thought. Mary Whitall Thomas was quieter and less vocal than her famous sister Hannah, but she too believed in women's rights. Carey therefore had a very staunch ally in her mother. Mother and daughter begged. They pleaded. They cajoled. Carey offered to complete four years of study in two years to save her father money.

Dr. Thomas refused. He had said no and he meant no. Had the education of a son been in question, the funds would have been found some way, but it was a foolish waste of money to educate a daughter.

Carey and her mother appeared to be beaten. What could they do next? Mary Thomas resorted to a final desperate strategy.

"Nothing is left for us but tears," she told Carey. "I have used every argument I can think of in talking with thy father. Reason will not move him. Now we shall see whether he can stand out against our weeping. We shall both have to cry day and night, thee as well as I."

Carey was ready even for that. So together and separately, they wept. And they wept. Her father pleaded with them, lost his temper, called them unfair, shut himself up, stayed away from home—all to no purpose. They accepted his reproaches in silence and in silence continued to weep whenever he appeared. Worried and distressed beyond endurance by their red eyes and wet faces, Carey's father surrendered at last.[1]

Carey went to Cornell University, graduating in two years by a herculean effort, as she had promised. She continued on to Zurich University in Switzerland to do graduate work and won the first summa cum laude to be granted to a woman there. She was appointed first dean and then president of Bryn Mawr College and became a legendary figure. She was one of the first women in this country to become president of an institution of higher learning.

Hannah would not be regarded as a genuine radical by today's feminists. She was too maternal ever to sacrifice her children to a career. But she was a crusader at heart and fought tirelessly against the evils of marriages as they existed in Victorian times.

Many problems of Victorian wives could be traced to what they called "demon rum," because husbands under the influence often turned into demonic brutes, abusing their families and drinking up the family income.

In April 1877, Hannah was attending a temperance meeting with a woman friend when she noticed a well-dressed young man coming in to the gathering. He stood at the back of the room, obviously quite sloshed, but his unfocused eyes were glued to the speaker. Apparently he was taking it all in.

When the speaker concluded with a heart-stirring plea, urging all present to sign the temperance pledge, the young man lurched up the aisle and signed. Then he collapsed on a front seat, sobbing piteously. Hannah and her friend immediately went to him.

"Does thee think we could take the poor fellow home?" whispered the other woman.

Hannah studied his face. He had an open, honest look despite a couple of days' stubble of beard. "Bring him along," she murmured.

And so the two middle-class ladies escorted the drunk to the Smiths' home in the very respectable section of Philadelphia. Hannah hoped fervently that none of her neighbors were looking out of the windows.

"Thank you so much for what you are doing for me." His voice was slurred, and he ended his sentence with an unmistakable hiccup.

"The Lord loves thee dearly and wants to see thee make a new start in life," Hannah replied firmly.

The three of them slowly ascended the outside porch stairs, one lady on each side of the dazed man, who was still quite unsteady on his feet. Once inside, the children appeared from everywhere and stared wide-eyed. Never before had they seen a house guest who was "under the influence."

First, Hannah and her friend fed him two hearty bowls of beef stew. The children lingered in the background utterly fascinated by the spectacle of a drunken person in their house. When the poor man began to sober up, the two women took him to the parlor.

The women got down on their knees and Hannah prayed. Completely undone by the pathos and fervor of her prayer, the man started crying again—great, maudlin sobs. Hannah got up and handed him her handkerchief and he gasped out a prayer himself. "Oh, Lord, I want to stop drinking; remove this curse from me." At that he stopped and blew his nose loudly before he went on. "Oh, God, I want to be good. Please, Jesus, make me good."[2]

Hannah and her friend were so affected by the young man's sincerity and brokenness that they asked the children to fetch blankets and pillows. After completing this task, the youngsters watched spellbound as the guest was tucked into bed on the parlor sofa. They all tiptoed out, and soon loud snores could be heard coming from that direction. When the man awoke, the temperance ladies were able to counsel and guide him toward a life of sobriety.

In November 1879, Hannah went to the national Women's Christian Temperance Union Convention in Chicago and helped elect her good friend, Frances Willard, as the president of the W.C.T.U. How much of a role Hannah played as a politician is not clear.

Susan B. Anthony joined them at one luncheon. How the air must have sparkled and crackled with the exchange of ideas among three of the greatest American women of the nineteenth century—Frances Willard, Susan B. Anthony, and the lesser known but equally potent personality, Hannah Whitall Smith.

Hannah took a preaching tour through the South early in 1884. On the first day of March she preached three times in Jacksonville, Florida. At 52, her energy and enthusiasm showed no signs of abating. Considering the fact that in Victorian times, very few women ever lectured publicly, much less preached, Hannah Whitall Smith must be regarded as both a daring innovator as well as a pioneer in women's rights.

12

Rebellious Daughter

The loss of four children had made Hannah Smith feel very insecure about her three remaining offspring. "To me the death of a child is the greatest wrench and grief the world can contain for a mother," she said once. "For it is an utterly irretrievable loss. Other losses can have their places supplied after a while, but the child's place is empty in this world forever."[1]

Soon after Ray's death in February 1880, Hannah wrote to her cousin Carrie saying that Mary was *so witchingly sweet and pretty that we do not any of us think she can live long.*[2]

On Mary's nineteenth birthday, her mother wrote her a "little love letter" in which she said, *I am thanking my heavenly Father for giving me such a gift as a daughter like thee. All thy life long thee has been nothing but a delight to me. I love thee, my precious, with an untellable mother love, and thee may always know this wherever or whatever happens. Moreover, I am on thy side against the whole world, and even against myself if this last could be possible.*[3]

In the fall of 1882, Hannah went to Northampton, Massachusetts, to visit Mary at Smith College and to help her fix up her room. Mother and daughter were standing in the somewhat bare dormitory room that contained a fireplace, bed, desk, and chest of drawers.

"Mother, I think some flowered curtains and a few brightly colored rag rugs would liven up this room." Mary, now a lovely sophisticated-looking young lady, was measuring the height of the window.

"Yes, yes, just what we need," nodded Hannah absently. She was thinking of bedcover and curtains to match, in a cheerful, colorful pattern and was mentally calculating the amount of material they would need.

"Mother, what shall I do with all these bare walls?" Mary asked.

"Some of the paintings thy father picked up on his western trip would do nicely."

Mary was deep in thought. "If only I could have a nice leather-covered armchair to sit here right by the fireplace. Then on cold nights I could have a really cozy place to do all the Greek translation that I must keep up with."

Her mother was beginning to see dollar signs in her head. Curtains, rugs, bedcover, and pictures from home were one thing, but a leather-covered armchair was quite an extravagance for an 18-year-old girl to have in her room at college. Hannah knew it was time to remonstrate with her daughter about economy and thrift.

Mary had opened the window to breathe the crisp fall air. The leaves had turned and a real New England autumn was spreading a riot of color all over the campus. It was such a beautiful, clear day that Mary leaned out of the window, entranced by the deep reds of the maple tree directly opposite her second-story room and the background foliage splendidly dressed in russet, saffron and sun-bright yellow. She inhaled deeply.

Suddenly Mary broke into a perfect paroxysm of coughing. Her mother ran to close the window and anxiously stood by her daughter until the cough finally wore itself out. Meanwhile, Hannah's vivid imagination started to work. Her precious darling had always had a weak throat.

For years she had feared that Mary would die of consumption, as tuberculosis was called then. Scenes flashed through her mind with amazing rapidity: Mary, lying on the bed, pale and thin, unable to control her racking cough . . . Mary, weak and emaciated, being held up by her mother as she continued to cough into her handkerchief, blood spurting out as the agonizing, painful hacking went on . . . Mary, lying lovely and serene in death in a filmy white dress with a beautiful, seraphic smile on her face.

Mary will be dead, and then how I will wish I had bought her that chair, Hannah thought. "No, I can't bear it," she said aloud.

Mary had recovered herself and was calmly putting her clean laundry in the chest of drawers. Startled by her mother's anguished cry, she glanced up to see Hannah clutch her hat and bag and hurry out the door.

"I will be back in an hour or two," she said, giving no explanation to the astonished Mary.

Hannah rushed out of the building, commandeered a ride in a public carriage that she found at the corner, and requested to be driven to the village of Northampton. Once there she marched into the nearest furniture store. Forthwith she bought the largest and most luxurious leather armchair that the proprietor had to offer and demanded to have it delivered to Mary's room immediately. The store owner was still in a daze as the impressive woman left as hurriedly as she had come in.

Two hours later there was a knock at the door of Mary's college room. Two burly men carefully carried in the large, comfortable chair. Mary stared at the expensive piece of furniture in open-mouthed wonder. Meanwhile her mother was beginning to regret her overindulgence. A mother should not be so foolishly prodigal. She should teach her daughter some discipline—some habits of thrift and self-restraint.

"There, daughter," she said somewhat grimly. "Thee coughed up that chair."[4]

Hannah's three children had distinct personalities of their own. Mary was tall, poised, and very attractive to the opposite sex. She was also an intellectual and seemed remarkably mature for her age. Her mother's eyes, so blinded by love, overlooked the fact that Mary was also quite a bit like her father. She spent money lavishly, was impulsive, self-centered, and spoiled.

Logan was a late developer. He didn't learn to read until he was ten and, as a boy, was mainly interested in dogs, loud noises, and sports. In his late teens, however, he began to develop intellectually and to manifest a real interest in the arts. He grew up to be a lover of beauty. Entering Haverford College in 1882 just before his seventeenth birthday, he was already developing the literary tastes for which he became known when he was older.

Alice began to be known as Alys around 1882 when she was fifteen. She was perhaps even more beautiful than Mary and was known for her sweet, unselfish nature. All the Smith children were tall and imposing figures; intelligent and handsome.

In 1882 when Mary was in her second year at Smith College, someone gave her a copy of Walt Whitman's book *Leaves of Grass* to read. She was warned that there were some "perfectly disgusting" parts to the book and was advised to skip over them. She discovered, however, "something sublime" in his poetry and wrote home about it. Mary was the darling of Robert's heart as well as Hannah's, and Robert invited the poet to visit them over Christmas in order to please Mary. Robert had never read a word of *Leaves of Grass*, but since Walt Whitman lived just across the river from Philadelphia in Camden, New Jersey, it was easy enough to bring him to Germantown.

Poor Robert never dreamed what a bombshell he was introducing into the quiet and respectable little conclave of Quakers in their neighborhood. The poet spent three days with the Smiths that Christmas and formed a lifelong friendship with all of them except Hannah, but he was especially fond of Mary. He called her his "bright particular star," and his correspondence with her has been preserved.

Hannah did not approve of Whitman, but was broadminded enough to welcome the controversial poet into their home. Her relatives, though, were horrified. Mary's aunt Sarah wrote her niece a scorching letter after the Christmas holidays, appalled that she would introduce such an immoral and disreputable character into the Smith household.

Curiously enough, the introduction of Walt Whitman into the family was the beginning of a trend. In the 1880s and 1890s, famous literary and intellectual characters drifted in and out of the Smith home. Some of them were radicals. Some were among the most outstanding opponents of Christianity in the nineteenth and twentieth centuries. Hannah listened to them tolerantly and went on placidly writing books glowing with faith—books that are still being sold and read today.

After Christmas of 1882, when Mary returned to Smith College, she wrote that she had begun to read and enjoy Herbert Spencer. Her mother was troubled. Mr. Spencer was a very persuasive agnostic. Hannah suddenly took the sleeper to Massachusetts to visit her daughter. Perhaps her indulgence and tolerance had gone a bit too far.

It was a cold winter morning and the two women were warmed by a roaring fire. Mary sat in her luxurious leather armchair while Hannah stood at the window, looking out upon the campus. The ice-coated dark branches of the maple trees twisted upward, silhouetted against the brilliant blue of the winter sky. A soft, downy snow had coated the ground.

"Daughter, is it necessary for thee to read Herbert Spencer?" Hannah said suddenly, turning from the window.

"Mother, there is no point in my getting an education if I am unwilling to explore new ideas."

"I know the arguments that Herbert Spencer makes," Hannah continued as she paced back and forth in Mary's room. "He says that the 'unknowable' cannot be comprehended by human reason. Since we can't know anything about God, even if there is such a being, we could not attempt to know what this being is like. Therefore, he says that the only reasonable belief is agnosticism."

"That's right," responded Mary. "And he also says that if there is a God, how did He come into existence? If He was created by something, then who created that? Could God have created himself? If He created himself out of nothing, then how can something come out of nothing?"

Hannah was becoming more and more agitated. "Thee must look at the outcomes of the two beliefs—agnosticism and a faith in Christianity. Looking the world over, thee will find that those who believe in a personal God are the good and the noble and the peaceful and the triumphant souls, while those who do not are the defeated and miserable ones."

Mary shook her head, almost imperceptibly. Then she rose from her chair to put another log on the fire.

"Take my case," Hannah continued. "All in me that is good comes directly from my belief in a personal God. And my greatest strength has come from my persistent holding on to this belief through days and months of fierce temptation to the contrary. Thy father gave place to doubt and is losing all sense of perception of God. Oh, my darling daughter"—there was a catch in Hannah's voice—"I have watched the growth and development of agnosticism in thy father. I can assure thee that it would almost break my heart to have my children travel on the same road."

"Mother, I could not stay in college and not be exposed to different forms of thought," Mary said with some impatience.

"In college, temptation is everywhere. I do not expect thee can escape it. But, my precious daughter, hold on to the God in whom thee has in the past trusted."[5]

"Father and I talked when he was here last month," Mary replied stiffly. "I told him that I have given up the idea of a personal God."

Hannah recoiled as if she had been struck. A look of infinite sadness came over her face. She crossed the room and knelt beside her lovely daughter, grabbing one of Mary's hands tightly. It was as if she were trying to pull her daughter back before it was too late.

When she could speak again, she said, "I beg of thee not to talk to Father about such things. His unbelief is contagious. Just last week as he was pouring out his lack of belief to me, I saw this beautiful picture of Christ as the liberator of women. Suddenly my whole heart went out to Christ in a perfect burst of love and loyalty. I was thinking of the dreadful bondage women are in all the world over and of how all the emancipation that has ever come to us has come through Jesus."[6]

Hannah pressed Mary's hand more tightly. "Do hold on to thy faith. Life isn't worth living without it." Then, seeing a completely blank expression on her daughter's face, she let go of Mary's hand. *Oh, Lord,* she prayed silently. *Thou must do it. Thou seest that I cannot.*

In the winter of 1883, Mary had left Smith College, returned home, and begun working for a kindergarten teacher's diploma. Meanwhile, she had become involved in several humanistic and scientific organizations. One was the American Association of Science. When it met in Philadelphia, arrangements were made for those attending from other countries to stay with local families.

Mary attended these meetings and offered to show visiting British gentlemen the sights of her home city. She took three of the visitors out to Camden, New Jersey, to call on Walt Whitman. One of these was a man named Frank Costelloe, an Irish barrister (lawyer) from London. He was ten years older than Mary, a bearded man of less than medium height.

Mary and Frank were instantly attracted to each other.

She found herself baring her soul, even sharing with Frank her fear that she had inherited the mental instability that ran in the Smith family. In his bouts of depression, Robert had a habit of reciting off a list of family mental disorders. Robert's attitude especially affected Mary, who was much like her father.

Frank, who was a Roman Catholic, was not the least alarmed. He told her that such fears were hogwash. He claimed that there were only four things that really mattered in human existence: God, duty, free will, and immortality. Mary found a great deal of security in Frank's calm assurance that he knew the answers to the riddles of life.

Costelloe returned to England, and Mary, joined by Logan, went to Harvard University. Since Harvard was just beginning to offer classes to girls, Mary became one of its first women students. The women's branch of the university, then called Harvard Annex, was later renamed Radcliffe College. Meanwhile, the romance of Mary and Frank continued through the mail. Finally, Frank proposed and Mary accepted by cable.

During this courtship, Mary led her parents to believe that she was seriously interested in her philosophy tutor, Mr. Palmer. Suspecting that Mary was in love with Mr. Palmer, Hannah invited him to Philadelphia for an inspection visit the Christmas of 1883.

Mary's use of the unsuspecting Mr. Palmer as a decoy totally took in her mother. A very curious document survives in Hannah's writing, a sort of manifesto written to Mr. Palmer, outlining her views on marriage. The young man, who was hoping to make Mary his wife, must have been a bit startled by his prospective mother-in-law's ideas. The letter, in part, read:

> *And now I want to take the opportunity to say a few words to you on the subject of marriage. As you have doubtless discovered, my daughters are far more to me than any other earthly consideration. I believe that motherhood is more of a passion with me than*

with most women. My ideal of marriage is an equal partnership, neither one assuming control over the other. Any marriage other than this is to my mind tyranny on the one hand and slavery on the other. I believe there ought to be an equal partnership in all property of incomes that accrue to them jointly after marriage and that each partner should have equal authority in disposing it. . . .

She went on to paint a grim picture of the tyrannies of the typical Victorian husband and then wrote:

I never could put into words how deeply I feel on this subject, nor how a woman's whole soul revolts from this position of slavery when once her eyes are opened to see it. It degrades and humiliates her in her own eyes with an anguish that no words can express. And I am convinced that most of the misery in married life arises from the fact that the soul of the woman is chafing against this degrading bondage.[7]

When the holidays ended, both Mr. Palmer and Hannah were in for a shock. Mary dropped her little bombshell and confessed her engagement to Frank Costelloe. Then she departed hastily for Harvard Annex where she soon received a barrage of protesting letters from both Robert and Hannah.

Not until Mary returned home for a spring break did Hannah have a chance to confront her daughter over the engagement. The two sat facing each other in identical platform rocking chairs in the parlor. It was late in the afternoon, and a dreary winter rain spattered the windows with droplets resembling tears.

Hannah shivered in spite of the warm fire in the stove. Her daughter had a set look on her face that the mother had come to dread. "Does thee know how upset thy father is over this engagement with Frank Costelloe? It has literally made him sick. He says that he will never give his consent because he sees marriage to Mr. Costelloe as a life of misery for thee."

Mary was very fond of her father, and she shifted uncomfortably in her chair. "But, Mother, I love him. I'll never love anyone else but him."

"But, my darling—thee doesn't know. Sometimes a sudden rush of love overpowers the best sense in the world for a while. And often during that senseless period, decisions are made that bring a lifetime of sorrow."

"That will not happen here," Mary went on. "I don't love Frank so much in a physical way as I do for his mind and his beliefs."

"Pshaw!" her mother blurted out, years of pent-up frustration over her daughter suddenly pouring out. "I know thee is physically attracted to him. And, Mary, I must confess to thee that I have made mistakes in thy training. And I am now deeply sorry for these mistakes. I should not have encouraged thy independence so much. To give a young person too much independence is like turning an engine loose without an engineer. A young person cannot know very much about life and its dangers, nor the paths that lead to pitfalls and precipices. Until they have learned, they do need guidance. Thee is so impulsively self-willed that thee cannot endure delay or opposition. I should have curbed thy self-will more." Hot tears welled up in Hannah's eyes.

Mary rose from her chair abruptly and turned her back to her mother. She stood by the window, such a slender, graceful figure, so achingly young and vulnerable. "I don't see what all this fuss is about," she said defensively. "I would have married someone, sometime. What is so terribly wrong with Frank?"

"What is wrong with Frank?" her mother repeated in amazement. "How could thee have been receiving our letters all winter and all the reading materials I have sent thee on marriages between Catholics and Protestants and ask that question? Hasn't thee paid any attention to our letters?"

"Yes, of course." Mary turned around to face her mother, impatiently brushing a strand of hair from her face. "But Frank is a liberal man. We will have no trouble."

"There is no such thing as a liberal man when a Roman Catholic marries a Protestant girl," Hannah fairly shouted. "I told thee about that niece of Laura Corse's who married an English Catholic. Her husband rules her with a rod of iron and has alienated her from her family and separated her from the children and made her life a misery to her. It is in the system of their church. Roman Catholic men are taught to keep their wives from having any liberty. The church itself will hound thee and make thee bring up all thy children to be Roman Catholic. The Protestant wife who lives with a Roman Catholic husband lives in a prison house."[8]*

Mary was still standing at the window trying to avoid digesting her mother's passionate entreaties. "Just because he is a Catholic doesn't mean that all Catholics tyrannize their wives. Frank isn't like that!"

Hannah groaned. "Thee hasn't had enough experience to know, as thy father and I know, what lies in store for thee in the future. Thee is blinded by love." The mother gripped the arms of her chair fiercely. "Dear daughter, I go to sleep praying for thee and I wake up praying for thee. If thee should end up marrying him, I should accept it as a death knell to all possibility of happiness for either thee or me. If it must be finally, I shall give thee up, as to a prison house, and shall spend the rest of my life trying to alleviate thy almost certain misery."[10]

---

*Author's Note: Back in the nineteenth century there was an impenetrable gulf between Protestants and Roman Catholics. At that time, the Catholic husband was very traditional. Backed by the church, he did insist on total obedience from his wife. Later on in her life, Hannah had an "opening," as she called her spiritual insights. She wrote to Mary in 1910: "I had one of my 'openings' in regard to Catholic ceremonies that took away forever my prejudices and made me feel that it was a fact that we are all one in God."[9] From her vantage point in 1885, though, Hannah was not overreacting when she viewed with great apprehension the prospect of her precious darling marrying a Roman Catholic. Almost all mixed marriages turned out to be misery for the Protestant wife.

Hannah rose unsteadily to her feet and grabbed Mary's hand. Turning her around, she held her in a tight embrace. "Oh, dear daughter," she choked out, "I beg of thee, do put off this marriage and give thyself more time to decide if this is what thee really wants."

Mary disentangled herself from her mother's arms and pushed her gently back into the chair. "All right, Mother," she sighed, "I will think about it."

Hannah had to be content with that. Mary would discuss it no further.

By the end of May it had become obvious that Mary was going to marry Frank. Hannah was in a state of despair. She had been suffering from chronic diarrhea (probably what we now call colitis) and was sleeping very little. Her hands shook so badly that she could barely write. Her religious friends were deeply concerned and added to her misery by telling her that if her faith were triumphant enough, she should not be sick.

Hannah confided by mail to Priscilla Mounsey:

> *They are so dreadfully down on me for being sick and scold me as if I were a great sinner. I am more puzzled than ever over it. It seems to me a dreadful thing to make all the poor, suffering invalids feel that they are yielding to the power of the devil in being sick, and that every pain they have is a sin. And I do not feel sure at all that good health is God's will for everybody, always.[11]*

By June, Hannah was close to the breaking point. The family was to embark for Europe on June 24 on the *Eider* of North German Lloyd Line. All the Pearsall Smiths were going to Mary's wedding. One night, several days before their departure, Hannah sat in her denuded "library," as she called the corner parlor where she did all her work and kept all her papers. The house was to be rented during their travels. Everything personal had been put away.

To Hannah it seemed as if her life were being packed

away, along with her notes for her latest book. She felt like a homeless wanderer being uprooted from her beloved Philadelphia and hauled off across the ocean to witness her darling daughter's execution. As Hannah settled back in her library chair, she remembered the words of a letter from her friend, Anna Shipley. Leaning forward, she extracted it from a box of mail carefully cataloged. Anna had written: *I awoke this morning with a strong impression of having had a dreadful dream about thee! And the words were ringing through me as if from some supernatural source: "There is a dreadful struggle going on in that family between the powers of good and evil."*[12]

Hannah let the letter fall to her lap and stared dully out the window. It was a lovely day in June. The earth was bursting forth in new life. The apple trees were clothed in pink blossoms. Roses were starting to bloom. She became vaguely aware of the contrast between the abundance of life outside and her own sense of being dead and lost inside.

Dear God, she prayed, *why is it that we lead and guide our children along until they grow up, and then they break our hearts? Why has thou allowed Mr. Costelloe to come into our lives and to tear my daughter away from my mother heart? . . . Oh, God, why do I have to suffer like this? I don't understand. Thou hast promised that all things will work together for good to them that love God, but I can't see how any good could come of this dreadful marriage. Oh, Lord, I've always been able to trust thee before. If thee doesn't help me, I am lost.*

The agitation in Hannah began to die down as she continued her prayer. *Thou doest all things well, and I will count on thee to get me over this hump. For I remember so well the lesson of the little bird and its song of hope in the midst of a dreary, desolate, cold winter.* Although all seems dark and wrong, and those we've trusted have failed us, and our prayers seem to go unanswered, yet there is still thee, oh God, who*

---

*at Nellie's funeral in 1857.

130

changes not, but is the same good, loving, tender God, yester-
day, today, and forever.

Although the fig tree shall not blossom, neither shall fruit
be in the vines; the labor of the olive shall fail, and the fields
shall yield no meat; the flock shall be cut off from the fold. . . .
Yet I will rejoice in the Lord, I will joy in the God of my
salvation.* And though thee slay me, yet will I trust thee.

When Hannah rose to her feet, there was a lovely peace
shining forth from her eyes, and a faint luminous smile
touched her lips. The Lord had brought her comfort, as
always.

Mary and Frank Costelloe were married in September
1885. Her mother said that her daughter "looked lovely and
was radiant with happiness." The young couple was hon-
ored by being invited to a wedding breakfast in Balliol Hall
at Oxford by the renowned Dr. Jowett. Frank had been a
protégé of his when the young man attended Oxford. After
the bridal pair had been toasted with lemonade and eulo-
gized with speeches, they rushed off to take the train to
London. Hannah returned to Philadelphia with Alys but
planned to travel back to London to help Mary furnish their
new home.

On September 13 she wrote to Mary: *Thee must have*
wondered how I managed to keep so cheerful on thy wedding
day when I expected to be so overwhelmed. The fact was, I
came to the conviction that it would be pure selfishness to
spoil thy happiness with my sorrow, that true love always
rejoices with those that rejoice and forgets self altogether.[13]

---

*Habakkuk 3:17–18, KJV.

13

Mary's Shocking Act

The marriage of Mary to Frank Costelloe changed the lifestyle of the Smiths considerably. Having come to terms with the reality of the situation, Hannah made regular trips by steamer back and forth between England and the United States in the years that followed. With the birth of Ray in 1887, she declared herself "a perfectly idiotic grandmother" and described little Ray as "a perfectly delicious baby girl."

Mary then found a house for her mother and father at 40 Grosvenor Road in London, four doors away from the house where she and Frank lived. By fall of 1888, Mary was pregnant again, an unwanted pregnancy. She was now bored with her marriage and her role as the wife of a rising politician.

In March 1889, Mary gave birth to a second girl, Karin, with Mother Hannah there to help. When Mary's recovery was slow, the Smiths discovered a country place called Friday's Hill near the Sussex village of Fernhurst where she could recuperate. It was a large, ugly house with ten acres of grounds and about two hundred acres of woodland. There were fourteen bedrooms, two coach houses, two cotages, a conservatory, billiard room, and tennis court. It was, in short, a typical English squire's house and became the Smiths' summer residence for many years.

Hannah appropriated for herself a little sewing room, which she named "The Last Resort." This was her special retreat. She would vanish into it whenever the *clash-ma-clavers* (as she called the gossip sessions and philosophical discussions of youth) became too much for her.

Robert waxed enthusiastic about Friday's Hill and strolled around the grounds in a Lord-of-the-manor style. He had a big sun-room built in the top of one of the trees on the grounds with a spiral staircase built around the tree as access. He called it his "Bo Tree," and intended to use it for Buddhist-style meditation. Hannah and Robert now had separate bedrooms and lived separate lives except when jointly involved in family and social activities.

At various times during the 1890s, a number of illustrious characters visited Friday's Hill. A roll call of their names read like excerpts from *Who's Who* in England and America: Beatrice and Sidney Webb, George Bernard Shaw, George Santayana, Mr. and Mrs. Oscar Wilde, and Bertrand Russell were all guests at one time or another, either at Friday's Hill or at the home on Grosvenor Road. The Pearsall Smiths even paid a call or two on the aging poet Tennyson.

During the summer of 1890, a gifted young man named Bernhard Berenson showed up at Friday's Hill. He had been at Harvard when Mary was there, and they had been introduced by a friend. Berenson was of Lithuanian-Jewish origin; his family had settled in Boston. After graduating from Harvard he was touring Europe, his trip financed by some wealthy sponsors who saw in him signs of genius. Falling in love with medieval and renaissance Italian art, he decided to devote himself to a lifelong study and interpretation of the painters of these periods. Mary had caught up with him on his return trip to England and invited him for a long weekend at Friday's Hill.

Everyone was impressed with the young man. Mary, in

particular, drank in Berenson's discourses on poetry, pictures, and music like a thirsty sponge. Here at last was the sort of thing for which her hungry heart had been yearning. She realized that a life centered around the search for beauty was the life she had always wanted. The combination of Berenson's personal charm and a doctrine that openly rejected Frank's political and religious ideals in favor of purely aesthetic ones could not have burst upon her at a more opportune moment.[1]

Mary spent all of August of 1890 with Bernhard—or "B.B." as he was called—visiting art museums and galleries around London. Her husband was also impressed with B.B., who began making frequent appearances at the Costelloe home at 40 Grosvenor Road. In September, the Costelloes traveled to Paris, where Mary met Berenson for a tour of the Louvre and other galleries while Frank visited with friends. The new world of art was an enchantment for Mary. When the Costelloes returned to London, Mary began an almost daily correspondence with B.B. She was not only attracted by his abilities as an art critic, but also found him physically alluring. He was an elegant, dapper little man, 25 years of age, with dark curly hair and soulful gray eyes.

At Christmas, Mary persuaded Frank to take her to Italy where she and B.B. spent three days visiting art treasures in Florence and Rome. In February, Bernhard came to England for several months, staying with the Costelloes before he found rooms of his own. The combination of daily proximity, physical attraction, and mutual infatuation with the arts was too much for Mary and B.B. They became lovers right under Frank's nose. Years later, Bernhard admitted to Mary's granddaughter that "I found myself in the classic French farce situation—hiding in a wardrobe, clutching my trousers, when Frank came home unexpectedly early."[2]

After Bernhard left England that summer of 1891, Mary found it intolerable to resume her former life. She decided, no matter what the cost, that she would leave Frank and go to Florence, Italy, to "study art" with B.B.

When the confrontation took place between Mary and Frank, the emotional fallout must have rattled windows in the whole London neighborhood. To Frank, divorce was unthinkable. Not only was he Catholic, he was in politics: A hint of scandal would end his career, and an errant wife who left her husband and ran off with another man was regarded as a totally depraved creature. Did Mary understand this? Mary did not seem to care what London society thought of her. She insisted on a separation of at least a year.

After several heated exchanges, Frank agreed on a plan that would enable him to keep his social position. He and Mary traveled together to Paris, where he remained while she went on to join B.B. and a friend in a tour of galleries throughout Germany. Mary was ecstatic. She "had happily cast off all concern for convention, and felt sure, with the optimism of a much-spoilt child, that she could pursue her own path undisturbed."[3]

Hannah was appalled. She totally disapproved of her daughter's action and supported Frank's position on divorce and the role of a mother in the home. Yet she loved her daughter, an all-out love that was mostly blind to Mary's shallow and selfish nature. Hannah and Robert had warned Mary that the marriage would become intolerable—yet now that it had happened, Hannah did not throw an "I told you so" at her daughter.

Mary, it seemed, was winning all the rounds. She and B.B. had a fling around Europe, then returned to Florence, where Mary moved into an apartment but a few doors from Bernhard. She had persuaded Frank to allow Ray and Karin to spend the winter with her. To top it off, her most respectable mother was also there for a month. Hannah somehow maintained the illusion that her daughter's relationship with B.B. was purely platonic, that Mary would return to London and her marriage at the end of the year. Mary, however, had found her niche. She had no intention of resuming her role as Frank's wife.

When Mary brought the children home to London and said she intended to go back to Florence, Frank's patience—whatever there was left of it—was exhausted. There were terrible scenes between him and his estranged wife. He was convinced that Mary, aided and abetted by her mother, planned to kidnap little five-year-old Ray. Finally the outraged husband made Mary sign a separation agreement that limited her visits to the children to four weeks a year and made her promise to be discreet about the whole affair so that his political reputation would not be damaged. Mary abandoned her children and returned to Italy.

At this point Hannah had a decision to make about involvement in her grandchildren's lives. Her daughter's behavior could well have instilled a sad "hands-off" policy toward her two grandchildren. After all, Frank had been the cuckolded party in this situation. He merited sympathy and certainly had a right to rear his children any way he wanted. Any role she might try to play as grandmother could be fiercely resented and resisted—it could be a no-win situation for her.

As for Mary, she had made the choice to abandon responsibility, violating everything her mother had taught her. Hannah believed the wife's duty was to remain with her husband, regardless—as she was doing with Robert. The hurt to Hannah was nearly unbearable. She very easily could have backed away from the mother-daughter relationship until Mary sought forgiveness for her folly. For the sake of her grandchildren, however—and also because of intense family loyalty—Hannah decided to be the intermediary in her daughter's marriage situation.

Since Frank was away from home a lot, Ray and Karin were in the care of their grandmother Costelloe, a cross, overprotective old lady who nagged the little girls constantly. Her attitude was so negative that nearly every form of innocent fun was forbidden to the children. Frank had also hired a nurse named Emma, who, it turned out, was even harsher on the children than the obdurate old lady Costelloe.

Since only a few houses separated the Costelloes and Smiths there on Grosvenor Road, frequent contact between the two families was inevitable, even though Frank Costelloe seldom issued any invitations. It was an awkward situation for Hannah, since she had to tiptoe around Frank to spend time with her grandchildren. She was constantly on edge, for fear Frank would take a sudden notion to banish her from their lives forever.

Once she was allowed to bring Ray back to her house for a little fun in the sunny nursery that Hannah had fitted up in the back of the house where the windows got the most light. When it was time for Ray to go home, the grandmother got the little girl's boots out and was tugging them on, preparing to go out in the rainy November afternoon.

"Grandma," Ray said, biting her little lip, "do I have to go home? Why can't I just live here with you?"

"Thee must be with thy daddy. Why doesn't thee want to live there?" Hannah asked gently.

"Because Nana (Emma) punishes me. She shuts me up in a dark room. She says you spoil me and she is going to take it out of me. She talks very cross to me."

"When did this happen?" Hannah asked mildly.

"It happens all the time."[4]

"Well, thee is very precious to me and I will do all I can to make thy life happy." The grandmother gave Ray a warm hug, set her on her feet, and walked her toward the door. "We must take thee back to thy house now." With the trusting little hand in hers, Hannah dutifully returned the child to her home.

Later Hannah stood at the nursery window, looking out on the dead grass and trampled, broken flowers that had turned brown in the frost. *How can I bear it?* she thought. *I feel sometimes as if it will kill me; only, alas! sorrow does not kill. So I will go down again tomorrow and protect little Ray all I can.*[5]

Not only Hannah, but Logan and Alys too became aware that little Ray was suffering from her nurse's cruel treatment. The three of them had a family conference and decided that Logan and Alys would confront Frank. Then, after the preliminaries were over, Hannah would join them. Accordingly, an appointment was set up with Frank. Logan, then 27, and Alys, then 25, marched to number 40 Grosvenor to do battle. Alys, prettier and softer spoken than her older sister, took a seat on an uncomfortable plush chair, so popular in Victorian times. Logan, often indecisive like his father, lounged beside her, sitting on a stool, a determined look on his face. Frank sat behind his massive desk.

"What was it you wanted to see me about?" Frank began, his voice testy.

Alys shifted nervously in her chair. "We are all concerned about Emma's behavior toward the children."

"Well, that is my business, isn't it?" he responded. "The children are my responsibility. I will do what I think best."

"We realize that," Logan chimed in, "but are you aware of how brutal she is to Ray? You are a busy man. You can't really be expected to keep tabs on the nursery night and day."

"Your mother has made me all too aware of her feelings in the matter," Frank continued coldly. "I must say that I find her constant interference most annoying."

"But Ray is your child. How can you stand by and allow her to be treated so harshly?" There was a note of pleading in the voice of the soft-hearted Alys.

"The children must be taught proper discipline," Frank continued. "They must be instructed by someone who has sufficient knowledge of the Catholic faith. I find Emma to be quite suitable." Then he glared at Alys and Logan. "You and your family have abrogated any rights to the children and their upbringing. I'm tired of your mother sneaking around, trying to impose on my good nature. I don't trust her in any way, shape, or form."

"Mother—sneaking around?" Logan was also upset. "In

all the years I have known my mother, I can testify to the unimpeachable integrity of her character!"

"The other morning she and the workmen whom she had hired barged into my house and removed my carpets before six A.M. when the rest of the house was soundly sleeping. I call that sneaking," said Frank crossly.

"But those were Mary's carpets," answered Alys in amazement. "I can remember when Mother bought those rugs for Mary and brought them here."

"According to English law"—Frank banged his fist on his massive desk for emphasis—"all the furnishings in this house are now my property. Neither your sister nor your mother has a right to a stick of furniture here. Why should I attempt to be conciliatory toward your sister and your mother when they keep conspiring against me?"

Logan opened his mouth to defend his mother, then gritted his teeth instead.

"Mary has hinted to me," Frank went on inexorably, "that she intends to institute legal action against me for refusing her access to her daughter. She threatens me with exposure and public scandal if I will not allow her to have Ray. She has no legal rights to either Ray or Karin. She has forfeited her right by her unseemly behavior. I have the law on my side. Furthermore, I have other plans for the children this summer. They will not be making their usual visit to Friday's Hill."

Alys began to cry quietly into her handkerchief. Logan was red-faced with anger. At this tense moment, Hannah was announced by the maid.

"Mother," Alys asked in a strained voice, "did thee come in with some men early the other morning and take up Frank's carpets?"

Hannah was appalled. "Of course I did not," she answered indignantly. "Mary must have ordered the men to take up the carpets. I knew nothing about it." Her level, honest gaze met Frank's. He tried to meet her eyes but failed, glancing downward with a trace of embarrassment.

"Well, Mary hinted in her last letters that you were going to create a public scandal if I refused to give Ray back to her," he said with some sulkiness.

"I would never consent to such a thing," Hannah replied. "I have tried to live my whole life in obedience to the Christian faith. Never in all my years have I handled any situation by resorting to force or threats!"

"Mother, Frank has said that he will not let Ray and Karin come to Friday's Hill this year," Logan said, watching his mother with anxious eyes.

The strain and anguish of the past months caught up with iron-willed Hannah. She broke down and started to cry. Then she pulled a handkerchief out of her reticule and vainly tried to stem the flood of tears. Logan and Alys both rose to their feet and went to her side. Logan patted her awkwardly, while Alys knelt down and put her arms around her mother's heaving shoulders. For some moments there was no sound in Frank's book-lined study except the almost hysterical sobs of Hannah, and Alys's soft little murmurs of consolation.[6]

Frank cleared his throat. "Perhaps I have been too hasty," he offered, trying to make amends. "We will discuss this again when we have all calmed down."

With Alys and Logan supporting their mother, the three of them retraced their steps to their own house.

Hannah slept very little that night. During the following week she wrote several desperate letters to Mary:

Now, darling, whatever it is that thee is contemplating, let me entreat thee to consider well before thee does anything that aggravates Frank. While we keep things on fairly friendly terms, we can have the children, but the moment he is angry, we shall lose them altogether. If they are torn away from us and left with Emma as an absolute tyrant over them, it will be too awful to endure. . . . It would be far wiser for thee not to stir him (Frank) up, both for thyself and for Berenson; for if he is made angry, he will bring a suit against thee for adultery with Berenson as co-respondent. That would certainly be very serious for B., especially as he has very compromising letters of B's which would be made public. Frank (naturally) feels very bitterly toward Berenson, and he said to me once that if matters come to an open issue he could and would ruin B.[7]

For a time after the tearful scene of January 12, Frank seemed to be more friendly toward Hannah and inclined to consult her about the children's welfare, but by March he was on the rampage again. Apparently Mary had written some letters to him that had made him very angry, and, as usual, Hannah was the victim of his fury. That Hannah's patience with her daughter was sorely tested is evident in this letter of March 21, 1893:

Frank says that he never wishes to stay in the same house with me and prefers to be independent as regards the children. . . . He is exceedingly angry with thee. . . . He shows us plainly that he is determined to go his own way and do what he thinks best for the children without consulting us. . . . I wrote thee a year ago that this would be the case if thee was not willing to make some sacrifices to keep thy hold on them. If thee would have been willing to give up Berenson—for a few years, at least—and keep thy hold on the children until they were old enough to understand things, all this might have been saved. Now I am afraid it is too late. . . . The law and public opinion as well would entirely support him in refusing thee access to (the children) while thee continues thy present relations with Berenson. It is literally and simply, I believe, a choice now for thee between the children and Berenson. . . . If thee realized the gravity of the situation and is willing to make some sacrifices in order to keep hold of thy children, there is, I believe, one way open to thee. Give up Berenson for a few years at least and come home. . . .[8]

A few days later Hannah sat at her desk and looked out the window toward the River Thames. The sun shone intermittently between banks of heavy clouds, scattering rays of diluted brightness on Vauxhall in the distance across the river. A spasm of pain tied her stomach into knots. She leaned back against her chair, and the sad thoughts rushed in upon her as inexorably as the heavy clouds moving outside her window.

"Alas for motherhood. How it hurts!" she said to herself. Like a malicious sprite knocking on the door of her mind came the memory of a dinner party at her sister's home in Baltimore in December 1886. She remembered with shame an embarrassing scene that had occurred in the midst of the meal. Edith Thomas, Hannah's niece-in-law, had remarked that Mary seemed to lead men on to fall in love with her. Hannah had turned on Edith in a burst of fury, insisting that Mary was an angel of goodness, using her power over men only to lead them to a higher and purer way of life. Hannah's tirade had caused Edith to leave the room in tears.

Tears stung the inside of Hannah's eyelids. How her mother love had blinded her to Mary's faults even to the point of defending her daughter's infidelities. She had sympathized with her daughter's unhappiness in her marriage with Frank, but she had never dreamed that it would all end like this. If only Mary had left Frank and come home with the children. If only Mary had not met Berenson. If only she had more sense of responsibility than desire for her own pleasure. Mary's youth had been so full of promise.

She then recalled sitting in that back room at The Cedars so long ago, in the summer of 1864, feeling such an overwhelming love toward the baby in the cradle across the room. She remembered the demure child of 10, posing for a portrait in London during their first preaching tour to Europe. How sweet and young Mary was, yet how poised and grown up. There was the little love letter she had written to her eldest on the occasion of her nineteenth birthday: *I am on thy side, even against myself, if such a thing could be possible.* . . .

She pressed her hands against her throbbing temples

and the tears flowed. "Alas for motherhood," she said to herself again. "How it hurts." Both she and Robert were to blame for the spoiled, wayward behavior of their daughter. They had indulged Mary too much as a child. They had thought Mary a paragon who could do no wrong. Now they were paying for their mistakes.

Oh, God, she cried out from the depths of her disturbed soul, *thou must help her. I cannot. Forgive me for my blunders. I trust her to thee. Thou art able to cover me for my foolish indulgence. I trust her and poor little motherless Ray and Karin to thy care. Thou lovest them far more than I do. Oh, Lord, I come to thee as a little child creeping into her mother's arms, longing for comfort. Thank thee for thy forgiving love.*

A wave of compassion flooded Hannah's troubled spirit. God's blessed solace surrounded her like a fortress. She felt herself enfolded in an embrace of consolation and sympathy. He was always there when she needed Him. She sat for several moments, savoring the assurance of the love of Jesus. Later she wrote that this thought was often to sustain her:

We are not wise enough to judge our situations, whether they are really in their essence joys or sorrows, but the Lord knows; and because He loves us with an unselfish and limitless love, He cannot fail to make the apparently hard or cruel or even wicked thing work together for our best good. . . .[9]

For whatever it would mean—and Hannah, to her credit, would not demand an answer from God—she would cling to God's love until the last.

14

Enter Bertrand Russell

Early one morning in October 1894, the front door of 44 Grosvenor Road opened and closed stealthily. In the parlor the front window curtains rustled as Hannah, now 62, and Alys, 27, peered furtively out of the window. Robert, who was almost 67 years old, had arrayed himself in his most fashionable clothes. He wore a dark velvet jacket, elegant striped trousers, spats over his shoes. A broad-brimmed hat of straw was perched jauntily on his bald pate. He carried a bouquet of autumn flowers. As the two women watched, Robert walked briskly down the street.

Robert was on his way to see a lady friend. When asked about the relationship, Robert blandly shrugged it off, calling her his "polished female friend."

"How intolerable it is!" Hannah said angrily to Alys. "Night and day he complains of his aches and pains. Yet look how frisky he is now."

"It's ridiculous," responded Alys. "Imagine having a mistress at his age." She placed a firm hand on Hannah's arm. "Mother, thee must leave it. There's nothing we can do but ignore it."

Hannah looked up at her younger daughter with tears in her eyes. "Oh, Alys, thee is such a comfort to me. Never did a mother have a dearer, more comfortable daughter than I have in thee."[1]

Alys was a help to her mother in numerous ways: She was expert at handling the capricious Frank; her tact and diplomacy won a place for her in his heart that had hardened against the rest of her family. She was patient with her father, no matter what her inner feelings were, and played word games (the forerunner of Scrabble) with him by the hour. Efficient and competent, she ran the household, relieving the aging Hannah of many of her domestic burdens. Soon, however, Alys's life was to be permanently and irrevocably changed.

Back in 1889, the first year that the Smiths had leased Friday's Hill, one of their prestigious local callers was the dowager Lady Russell, widow of Lord John Russell, who had been prime minister earlier in the century. Lady Russell had been staying with her son Rollo, whose household was located near Friday's Hill. Upon first acquaintance Hannah referred to the elderly woman as a "delightful old lady." She was later to revise her opinion.

In that same summer of 1889, the grandson of Lady Russell came with his Uncle Rollo to call on the newcomers at Friday's Hill. Bertrand Russell, then 17 years of age, was enchanted with Alys Pearsall Smith. Still a shy schoolboy, his eyes glowed with admiration for the 22-year-old college student from America. He found Alys not only beautiful but also more emancipated than any English young ladies of his acquaintance. Some time after that, Bertie (as he was known to the family) documented his thoughts on his first encounter with Alys: *She was kind and made me feel not shy. I fell in love with her at first sight. I did not see any of the family again that summer, but in my subsequent years during the three months that I spent annually with my Uncle Rollo, I used to walk the four miles to their house every Sunday, arriving to lunch and staying to supper.*[2]

Alys had continued to be friendly and made the stiff, reserved boy feel at ease. Nevertheless, it wasn't until 1893, when Bertie was 21 and fast making a name for himself at Cambridge as an intellectual, that he and Alys began to entertain serious thoughts toward each other. B.R., as he was also called, had had a most disagreeable and constricting early life. His parents died when he was little more than an infant. Reared by his grandmother and a maiden aunt, he had been educated at home in Pembroke Lodge, a house on the edge of Richmond Park that Queen Victoria had deeded for life to Lord John and his wife.

Lady Russell was a notable character—often referred to when her husband was prime minister as "the Deadly Nightshade" because of the malignant influence she supposedly wielded over her husband. Pembroke Lodge was a terrible environment for a sensitive and highly intelligent little boy, who grew up lonely and solitary, isolated from other children. The old Lady Russell and her unmarried daughter, Agatha, subjected little Bertie to an unnatural, stilted Victorian piety.

Alys found Bertie congenial when they started courting in 1893. She was nearly as priggish as he. They discussed philosophical subjects for hours and began to write each other when they were apart. The courtship flourished as 1893 gave way to 1894. In February, Alys admitted that she loved him. Although they had conducted their relationship very circumspectly, almost secretly, Bertie's grandmother found out in March 1894. She hit the ceiling.

Bertie was summoned to Pembroke Lodge. He found his aunt and his grandmother waiting for him in the stiff, starched parlor with grim, set faces.

"Bertie, what is this I hear about you and that low-class American adventuress?" The crisp, cultured voice of his grandmother was icy.

"Grandmother, you met the Pearsall Smiths years ago at Friday's Hill. I was under the impression that you liked them," the young man said meekly.

"I was doing my duty and being civil to my neighbors. Good manners demanded that I welcome them to Fernhurst," replied Lady Russell sternly.

"I seem to remember your saying that you found them to be quite refined and genteel for Americans." Bertie struggled to hold his composure.

"I did find them pleasant, superficial acquaintances—but this is different. This young woman is obviously taking advantage of your youth and inexperience to get herself a titled husband. Americans will do this sort of thing, you know," she said grimly.

"If you knew her better, Grandmother, you wouldn't say such a thing!" Bertie burst out. "She is as pure and guileless as any girl I ever met."

"What do you know of the world, my dear boy? She is years older than you, and you know little of the ways of experienced women of the world. Alys Pearsall Smith is nothing but an unscrupulous baby snatcher!"

Bertie gazed at his indignant grandmother and his silent but equally disapproving aunt in horror. "I simply will not let you talk this way about a sweet, earnest, sincere, truthful person like Alys," he managed to blurt out.

"Consider this, Bertie," his grandmother snapped. "You would not dare to bring her into our social circle. Her vulgarity would perpetually put us to shame!"[3]

Bertie had taken all that he could endure. He could not stand another moment of this abuse of the lovely Alys. Yet he had been a dutiful and cowed child in that dreary household too long to act as rude as he was feeling. "I am a man now," he said firmly. "I must pursue my own course in life." With that he rose from his chair, walked over to the two elderly women, gently brushed their papery-thin cheeks with his lips, and left the room.

Lady Russell continued to try to sabotage the relationship, especially after Bertie and Alys became engaged in April 1894. When she discovered that overt opposition was not working, she resorted to more subtle methods. There was, she said, insanity on both sides of the family. Bertie's father had been an epileptic, Aunt Agatha's engagement to a young curate, many years before, had been terminated because of her insane delusions. Bertie had an uncle in a mental hospital.

All of this was a terrible shock to the young Russell, who had never heard all these facts before. Then the old lady slyly pointed to the mental cases among the Pearsall Smiths, not exactly news to Alys, who had grown up listening repeatedly to Robert's morbid litany of all his mentally disturbed relatives.

Lady Russell also mentioned somewhat venomously the rumors circulating to the effect that Mary was insane. "Surely no woman in her right mind would run off from her husband and abandon her children." These attacks from Bertie's grandmother prompted another pleading letter from Hannah to Mary: *Lady Russell is saying that Father is insane and that thee inherits it, which is the reason thee has forsaken thy husband and children. . . . The fact is, to have the taint of insanity fastened on a family is a far worse misfortune than almost anything else in the world. It would blight poor little Ray and Karin as they grow older, and it bids fair now to put an end to Alys's happy prospects.*[4]

Hannah then went on to try to persuade Mary to take an apartment in Paris, away from Bernhard Berenson— feeling that if Mary did this, Frank Costelloe might then be persuaded to let her have the children. *We could then point to this fact and say, "You see, she cannot be insane or Mr. Costelloe would not let her have the children,"* she wrote. *It will be a very serious thing for thyself, not to mention thy children or Alys, if this taint of insanity gets fastened on them.*[5]

Mary was apparently unmoved by the desperate pleas of her mother. She had no intention of leaving Berenson: Anonymous reports of her insanity circulating around England did not appear to trouble her very much.

Meanwhile, Lady Russell was milking the insanity possibility to the utmost. After Bertie had graduated with highest honors from Cambridge in the summer of 1894, she hustled the young couple off to a number of eminent medical specialists, hoping that professional opinions would scare them into canceling their engagement. The old lady made their lives so miserable that Bertie and Alys decided to marry anyway, but made a vow not to have any children.

The wedding was set for just before Christmas 1894, but Lady Russell never stopped trying to thwart their plans. She complained that worry over her precious grandson had brought upon her a "disease like cancer," and through her doctors she got Bertie and Alys to agree to a three-month separation. Young Russell left England for Paris in September, with the understanding that he and Alys would marry immediately on his return.

Meanwhile, Alys and her mother visited Pembroke Lodge to discuss wedding arrangements. Lady Russell, who was still not reconciled to what she regarded as a deplorably unsuitable match, was inexcusably rude to Hannah.[6]

Nevertheless, the Honorable Bertrand Russell and Alys Pearsall Smith were married at the Quaker Meeting in Westminster in London on December 13, 1894. Lady Russell and Lady Agatha did not attend.

In February 1895, Hannah wrote a poignant letter to her newly wed daughter, eloquently urging Alys to hold on to her faith. In this letter she quoted from an old family friend who, when she heard of Alys's marriage, had said, *I trust and assume she has married a Christian man who loves the Master's work. How else could they walk together?*[7]

In her letter to Alys, Hannah reminded her: *From thy babyhood thee has always seemed to have an instinctive perception of spiritual things. . . . Thee was evidently a born Christian philosopher, able as a baby to take the philosophical view of things and of life. Tell Bertie he must not upset this spiritual foundation of thy character by any of his speculations. And thee must guard it, precious daughter, as one of thy most sacred possessions.*[8]

How unfortunate for Hannah. Trying to keep her children from straying from their beliefs was like trying to stop an avalanche with two bare hands. Unbelief dominated the intellectual, literary, and artistic circles with whom Mary, Logan, and Alys traveled. Logan claimed to have lost his faith as a boy of 11, sitting in a cherry tree. Mary claimed that her unpleasant experience with Frank's Catholicism was cause enough for her to bail out of Christianity altogether. Alys married a brilliant and articulate atheist—and her faith did not last more than a month after their marriage.

Prominent leaders and writers rejected Christianity in large numbers during the period from 1890 to 1940. The wife of C.S. Lewis, who was born during this time, said that she had grown up in a generation that "sucked in atheism with its canned milk." None of those who disdained the Christian faith, least of all the supremely gifted Bertrand Russell, realized that Christianity was the glue by which Western civilization was held together.

It was one of the strangest ironies, that Bertrand Russell, one of the most outspoken and persuasive atheists of the twentieth century—author of the atheist's bible, *Why I Am Not a Christian*, the man who said that he would not believe in God unless he heard voices from the heavens—would be the son-in-law of Hannah Whitall Smith, one of the most persuasive advocates for Christianity during this period.

Perhaps it was inevitable that Bertrand Russell came to despise his mother-in-law almost as much as he did her Master.

15

Grandmother

Having seen Hannah through numerous periods of blackness, it may be hard to believe—but the decade of the 1890s was by far the worst period of her life. Robert's blatantly immoral behavior angered her. Lady Russell's opposition to the marriage of Bertie and Alys chafed her. Mary's stubborn refusal to return to her children grieved her.

Nevertheless her indomitable, adventurous spirit managed to survive.

Things loosened up considerably in the Costelloe household by 1894. Emma had left and her place had been taken by Miss Claire. Miss Claire was not Hannah's favorite person in the whole world, but the two women managed to get along. Thus Hannah was able to spend more time with Ray and Karin.

Hannah brought joy and adventure into their lives to such an extent that after she died, Ray wrote a little book called *A Quaker Grandmother*. This little volume is full of the unselfish, loving side of Hannah, especially in her behavior toward the children.

In the mid-1890s, Hannah's niece, Grace Thomas Worthington, fled to England from an unhappy marriage, bringing her three children. The fatherless family settled near the Smiths. Fortunately, Grace's children were close to Ray and Karin in age. The five children became close friends.

One day they all had set their hearts on having a real live elephant for a pet. The indulgent Grandma Smith was called upon to produce the elephant. Hannah actually drove her carriage to Whiteleys retailers (who advertised they would provide anything on earth) to ask them to hire an elephant for her little dears. When she discovered that the huge animal had to be fed a ton of hay each day, Grandma decided to buy toy elephants instead. This was one of the few times Ray could remember her grandmother disappointing their expectations.

Sometime in 1894, when the family had gone to Friday's Hill for the summer, Ray and Karin, now seven and five, persuaded 62-year-old Hannah to climb a haystack. The hay in the meadows of Friday's Hill had been put in huge stacks, as was the English custom. One of the stacks was put under a heavy tent cloth until there was time to thatch it with straw. The children climbed the ladder against the side of the haystack, using it as sort of an aerial playhouse. The tent cloth was stretched high enough above the top of the hay so that there was a kind of secret hidey-hole in between. Nothing would do but for Grandmother to climb the ladder and experience the joys of haystack living. So poor Hannah hoisted her stout, complaining, arthritic old body up the ladder to the hidey-hole and sprawled on the hay.

Several years later, Ray and Karin talked their grandmother into taking them to the Earl's Court Exhibition in London. At the exhibit was a water slide that the little girls found delightful sport. Of course Grandmother must be persuaded to try it too. So there was the 66-year-old Hannah with her stately black gown and her little lace cap zooming down the water chute with eleven-year-old Ray and nine-year-old Karin. Hannah's "inside self" usually got the better of her creaky old joints, for she was unable, as she had been so many times before in her life, to resist trying a new experience.

The British, not having any Fourth of July to celebrate, had to resort to setting off fireworks on Guy Fawkes Day. Year after year, Grandmother Smith could be seen on her balcony on Grosvenor Road "resolutely setting off rockets and Roman candles, her serene Quaker face shining incongruously in their lurid light. The five children danced like five savages around her. The young ones loved the smell of gunpowder that made her drawing room almost uninhabitable for days and believed that Grandmother really loved the smell too."[1]

In the 1890s, Hannah was still very much the crusader. She wrote one friend: *This May I found myself booked day after day for one meeting after another. And now, June threatens to be almost as bad: From the 14th to the 24th we are to have one continuous string of meetings every day and all night long in connection with the world's W.C.T.U. I wonder how many of our tombstones will have the epitaph, "Died of Too Many Meetings"?*[2]

Though Hannah could be patient and forbearing toward disagreeable people, she had a very short fuse whenever she encountered injustice of any kind. Once she was driving in a carriage along a crowded London street. At this time she was a stout, middle-aged lady, dressed in black, with her white lace cap on her head. Suddenly she saw on the sidewalk a young bully abusing a smaller child. Without waiting for the carriage to stop, she jumped out with umbrella in hand and began to rain blows on the bully, subjecting him to a fierce tongue-lashing at the same time. The bully fled.

Another incident occurred at Friday's Hill. The Smiths were popular with their neighbors and frequently had visitors. On this particular occasion, some visiting neighbors brought a young man to tea.

It was a decorous gathering. The ladies and gentlemen

were distributed around the large parlor. The ladies wore wide-brimmed hats, most of them trimmed with flowers. They had on gloves and carried parasols. A maid was circulating with trays of watercress and cucumber sandwiches and scones. Mary was presiding over the teapot, pouring from a graceful silver urn into fragile china cups. There was a murmur of polite conversation throughout the room as several clusters of guests and family members gathered into different groups to share genteel gossip about the weather, the crops, or the latest action of parliament.

Hannah was seated at the edge of a group of young people and was trying to listen to a querulous old lady on her right, who was boring her hostess with a seemingly endless catalog of her aches and pains. The visiting young man, who had been brought there by her neighbors, had his back to Hannah. During a lull in the conversation, she heard his somewhat strident voice bragging to Alys.

"When I was over in Africa," he said in the casual, clipped accent of what the British call a "public school" voice—meaning that he had probably attended Eton or Harrow—"I had a jolly good time."

"Tell me about it," said Alys politely. Alys was always kind, even to bores.

"One day," he continued, "I was stuck sitting on a riverbank near the coast, waiting for the guides to repair our canoes. It was terribly hot and muggy, don't you know, and I was bored. Fortunately I had my trusty little pistol with me. I began taking potshots at the niggers on the opposite shore of the river. Terribly entertaining, don't you know, seeing their frightened leaps and jumps as they faded into the jungle. I never laughed so hard!" And he chortled loudly.

He could not see Hannah's face as he related this tale. She had turned quite pink. Dressed in her usual stately black gown, she rose majestically and limped over to stand face-to-face with the young man.

"You dare to call yourself a civilized Englishman," she began, her eyes shooting out sparks. "How can you sit here and brag so casually about shooting at human beings just like yourself who were simply minding their own business?"

She barely paused for breath. "Talk about the 'white man's burden,' " she sputtered, using a familiar imperialistic slogan of the day, "those so-called ignorant savages can hardly be as ignorant and savage as you, young man!"

The face of the Englishman was crimson now, and the room was so quiet everyone could hear Hannah's heavy breathing. The angry warrior was not finished. "I can hardly imagine more disgraceful behavior from someone who regards himself as a member of the British upper class. And what makes you"—and she pointed an accusing finger at the squirming victim—"think that in the sight of God, you are any better than those unfortunate natives whose lives you hold in such little esteem? To God, they are every bit as precious as human beings as the most privileged peer in England.

"Young man," she finished with a fine flourish, "you are cowardly, unsportsmanlike, and certainly no gentleman. I request that you leave my home at once."

The fatuous young man, demolished by one of Hannah's famous steamroller tirades, fled. In total disgrace, he hid out in his cottage for the remainder of his visit, not daring to show his face again.[3]

16

The Iniquitous Will

The tragedy of Robert Pearsall Smith continued through the 1890s. Robert's death wish took several forms. He talked often about death and pictured himself on his deathbed. Then, early in 1895, he had an attack that he was certain meant he was going to die. He even went so far as to wash his feet, preparatory to being laid out.

Five days later, still very much alive, he announced that he had cancer of the stomach. His wife reported to Alys, "The truth is that Robert has been eating enormously all winter and simply had a serious attack of indigestion. One's sympathies are dried up when people make such a fuss over themselves."[1]

On February 2, 1895, in a letter to Alys: *Father has had a severe attack of nervous dyspepsia and has died in imagination over and over! I never was more glad that thee was married and well out of it than when I saw what we were likely to have to go through as he grows older and more infirm.*[2]

In 1897, Robert went off to the south of France and became seriously ill with influenza. Logan rushed to his bedside.

He found his father lying pathetically in bed like a sick animal, muttering to himself his usual boring litany of platitudes, grievances, and boasts. Somehow he recovered and Logan managed to get him back to London.

Then in April 1898, Robert's death wish was granted. He passed away. The cause remains a mystery since nothing seems to be recorded about it. Mary's comment was that she couldn't help feeling that he would be taking "a great interest in the disposal of his body—trotting around himself to give the last touches."[3]

Hannah treated the whole event calmly, as she did the deaths of all elderly people. She had a disconcerting habit of congratulating her friends when any aged relative was "safely gathered." She answered some letters of condolence from a friend, saying: *Thy dear letters have been a great comfort to me. They express so exactly what I feel myself, and confirm me in the strong sense I have had ever since my dear husband was permitted to escape from the earthly tabernacle, that his long time of darkness is over and that God's light has shone upon him at last. I have always felt sure his clouded spiritual life was the result of physical causes and I believe it was truly the "binding of Satan" from which deliverance has come. He has reached Home and can now understand the way that seemed so dark to him while he was walking in it.*[4]

Perhaps this was wishful thinking on Hannah's part. She continued to believe that all God's children were "safely gathered."

In the summer of 1899, Frank Costelloe had to have an operation on his ear and jaw. He had developed cancer of the ear and by October was quite ill. Hannah was genuinely sorry for the sick man and admired his courage in facing up to his illness. She was also beginning to have a serious concern about what disposition he had made for Ray and Karin.

She was quite right, as it turned out, to be troubled about the future welfare of the children. In between bouts of cancer, Frank made a new will. Shortly after this, on a blustery fall day, Hannah had a visitor, a Roman Catholic priest named Father Brown. Father Brown was ushered into Hannah's parlor, where she joined him.

Father Brown started the conversation. "Mrs. Pearsall Smith, I realize that my visit to you at this time might be deemed highly irregular. Actually, I am breaking a confidence in presenting myself here. However, in order to be true to my God and my own best impulses, I felt that I must come to you at once."

"Well, I'm sure you* have done the right thing. Ultimately we are answerable only to our God," Hannah said with an encouraging smile.

Father Brown swallowed nervously. "I have been appointed one of the five guardians of your grandchildren in the will recently drawn up for your son-in-law, Mr. Benjamin Francis Costelloe."

He really had Hannah's attention now.

"I studied the matter deeply and committed it to God in prayer, and I have come to the conclusion that I must reveal to you the contents of this will. I believe that the document is most iniquitous and will definitely put your grandchildren, Ray and Karin, in jeopardy."

Hannah's heart began to race as she studied the face of the Roman Catholic priest.

"In his will, Mr. Costelloe has appointed five Catholic guardians—two of us priests," continued Father Brown. "He has arranged that Karin and Ray are to live in cheap lodgings under the care of their governess who, as you know, is a young, ignorant, convent-bred German girl whom the children have only known for a short time. As you also know, this girl is barely twenty-one and knows little of the ways of the world. According to the terms of the will, neither Mr. Costelloe's estranged wife—your daughter Mary—nor any of the rest of your family is to have

---

*In her later years Hannah began dropping the "thees" and "thous" from her speech, especially with strangers.

any say in the future life of your grandchildren. You are specifically to be excluded as guardians. Ray and Karin are to continue to attend the school that he has chosen. They are to receive very little education and are to be prepared to earn their own living when about 16."

Hannah was appalled at this information. All color drained from her face. For a few moments there was complete silence in the parlor, punctuated only by the loud ticking of the officious-looking grandfather clock standing against the wall behind the priest. At length Hannah recovered herself. "Father Brown, I think it was a courageous and gentlemanly thing for you to come here and disclose to me the terms of my son-in-law's will. I will never cease to praise our mutual Father in heaven that He brought you here."

"The more I prayed about the matter," Father Brown spoke warmly, "the more convinced I was that you should learn the terms of this will before it was too late. I couldn't believe that it was God's will for these dear children to be consigned to the care of comparative strangers and separated from their own beloved family."

"My dear man, I will never be able to thank you enough for your sincere regard for Ray's and Karin's well-being," Hannah responded. "Had my son-in-law wished to consign his children to certain ruin, he could hardly have devised a better plan. And I can only think in charity that the cancer had affected his brain and that he really did not know what he was doing."[5]

"I am sure that you will make good use of this information. My prayer is that the dear little girls will have a happier fate than their father had in store for them," he said, rising to leave.

Hannah rose also and shook the priest's hand. "You have won my everlasting gratitude," she said. "You are indeed a true follower of Jesus."

On the advice of a solicitor, the Smiths moved quickly to have the two children declared Wards in Chancery. One of the special functions of the Chancery Court was to protect children whose future might be in jeopardy. Having Ray and Karin declared Wards in Chancery simply meant that they were under the court's protection. Nothing could be done to them or with them without the consent of the court. Any child could be made a Ward on the payment of one hundred pounds by anyone who was willing to pay the money. The action could be done without the knowledge of the parents or relatives. Once a Ward, the child had to remain a Ward until he or she was of age and could claim the protection of the court at any time.[6]

Frank Costelloe died of cancer of the ear on December 22, 1899, at age 44. Within an hour of his death, Hannah and Mary—who had returned to England as Frank lay dying—had applied to the presiding judge at the Chancery Court and had the necessary legal steps taken.

Also within an hour after Frank's death, the children were whisked off to 44 Grosvenor Road. Once there, under the jurisdiction of the Pearsall Smith family, a court order was needed to dislodge them. It wasn't long before the Catholic guardians that Frank had appointed for Ray and Karin became aware that they had been outwitted by the Smith family.

Dr. Flanagan, the most prejudiced of the five guardians, paid a visit to Hannah's home shortly thereafter, where he was received by Mary.

Dr. Flanagan's Irish face was purple with rage. He could hardly speak. "You . . . you . . . you *infamous* woman!" he sputtered.

"I'm afraid I fail to understand—what you are referring to," Mary replied coolly.

"You know perfectly well what I am talking about!" the choleric man fairly screamed. "You and your interfering old mother and that 'honorable' sister of yours have connived and veritably kidnapped the children of my poor departed friend, Mr. Costelloe." Dr. Flanagan's hands were clenched. The veins in his forehead and neck were distended, so that he looked as if he were about to have a stroke.

"You shall pay for this infamy," he sputtered on. "Sneaking two helpless children out of Mr. Costelloe's house not ten minutes after he had breathed his last breath. Have you no respect for the dead?" His clenched hands were beating a tattoo on the arms of the chair, his eyes were bulging from his inflamed face.

I wonder if I should summon Mother, Mary was thinking. *Poor Dr. Flanagan is working himself into a terrible frenzy. It is really quite alarming.* She sat there in silence, looking dismayed at the frightening spectacle.

Dr. Flanagan rose from the chair, so infuriated that he was unsteady on his feet. He paced back and forth in the cluttered room like a caged beast. He went past the umbrella stand and started to grab an umbrella. Mary shrank back into her chair. He seemed perfectly capable of beating her to death.

"Dr. Flanagan"—she hoped her voice wasn't quavering—"I think you had better go now. This whole issue will be decided by a court of law. It matters very little what your personal opinion is, or mine. This is a legal matter. I will see you in court."

The good doctor opened his mouth to bluster some more—then closed it again, directing toward her one last poisonous glance as he stomped out of the room. He let himself out the front, closing the door behind him with an unforgettable slam that seemed to rock the house to its very foundations.[7]

Hannah and Mary, of course, contested the will, asking the court to have it set aside. Meanwhile, the little girls were safe at Grosvenor Road.

Father Brown and the other priest sided with the Smiths, but Dr. Flanagan and the two Catholic ladies who comprised the rest of the five guardians were determined to carry out the provisions of the will. Litigation went on for nearly a year, causing Hannah mounting legal fees and many nerve-racking months of worry and suspense.

Meanwhile, they had possession of the children, and Hannah was prepared to take drastic action to keep them— even if it meant going to prison. Grandmother Hannah worked herself into such a state over the court trial that she would lie in bed at night and make up paragraphs to be sent to the papers about the unfairness of the patriarchal system that could snatch children away from their mother and grandmother and consign them to a life of misery and deprivation.

Fortunately, there was no need to resort to such dramatic measures. After endless arguments between the lawyers of both parties, the "other side" at last became convinced that such an iniquitous will would be sure to be set aside by the judge. Influenced by the two sensible priests, all the guardians appointed in Frank's will were persuaded to join with Hannah and Mary in asking the judge to make Hannah the acting guardian and to give her the custody of the children. In return, the Pearsall Smiths had to promise that the children would be brought up as Catholics and that nothing would be done by Hannah or anyone else in the family to undermine their faith in that church. The final agreement stipulated that the Chancery Court must oversee Hannah as guardian until the children became of age and that the girls could not go outside the jurisdiction of the court (outside England) without the permission of the Chancery Judge.[8]

The next act in the drama was set in Italy. There, Mary and Bernhard Berenson decided to get married. Hannah accordingly secured permission from the Chancery Judge and brought Ray and Karin to Florence in December 1900. The wedding took place in the chapel of the elegant Florentine villa named *I Tatti*, which the Berensons had leased as their future home. Thus were all the loose ends of the terrible 1890s tidied up.

After the wedding Hannah took the girls back to London and established a permanent home for them there. Mary, though her top priority was still Bernhard and their life in Italy, made frequent visits to London to see her children and spent a good part of every summer at Friday's Hill.

The entire decade had been an agonizing and frenetic time for Hannah. As she looked back on those disturbing days in later years, she was to say that her principal memories of the house at Grosvenor Road were years of misery that she endured there with the children when they were in Frank's clutches, and years of disgust as she watched Robert sneaking out of the house to go to his mistress.[9]

Despite the enjoyable times she had with her grandchildren and her continuing public appearances, she sometimes longed for a "blessed release from a life that seemed hopelessly entangled and from which she could see no relief."

In the midst of all the upheaval and heartbreak, she wrote a little book called *Everyday Religion*. In it she summed up the faith that sustained her in the height of her tribulations:

> *God alone is unchangeable. What we call "spiritual blessings" are full of the element of change. The prayer which is answered today may seem to be unanswered tomorrow. The promises, once so gloriously fulfilled, may cease to have any apparent fulfillment. The spiritual blessing which was at one time such a joy may be utterly lost. Nothing of all we once trusted in and rested in may be left us but the hungry and longing memory of it all. But when all else is gone, God is still left. Nothing changes Him. He is the same, yesterday, today and forever, and in Him is neither variableness, nor shadow caused by turning. And the soul that finds its joy in Him alone can suffer no wavering.*
>
> *"And ye now therefore have sorrow: but I will see you again, and your heart shall rejoice, and your joy no man taketh from you" (John 16:22).*[10]

17

God Is Enough

After celebrating her sixty-ninth birthday on February 7, 1901, Hannah wrote this to her friends:

There is one thing which the death of my son-in-law, Frank Costelloe, has accomplished and which I do not believe anything else could, and that is it has made me want to live! I feel as if I will really be needed for about ten more years to maintain an English home for my grandchildren and to avoid the complications that would inevitably arise in regard to their guardianship if I should die.

I confess it feels very funny to want to live after having so long looked forward with such an eager desire to go. However, so it is, and I give you liberty to wish me many happy returns on my future birthdays—or rather I should say ten happy returns, for in ten years both Ray and Karin will be of age and will be free from the Chancery Court and from all danger of interference by any opposing guardian. If you had only known this when you wrote me those lovely letters on my 69th birthday, you might have freely wished me those ten happy returns. . . .[1]

It was curious that in this letter, Hannah predicted

164

within a few months her remaining years on earth.

Though lame with arthritis, Hannah still went everywhere, using a cane when necessary. By 1903, she could barely hobble, so she was wheeled about in a bath chair (the forerunner of the wheelchair). She was, however, enjoying life greatly and her sense of humor really flowered as she grew older.

Meanwhile, Ray and Karin were attending Kensington High School, a good, modern-day school in London, and living with their grandmother at Grosvenor Road. Logan, Alys, and Bertie were nearby.

All was not going well with the Russells. Although Alys adored her husband and did throughout her life, Bertie was beginning to find her irritating. By 1902, he had admitted to Alys he no longer loved her. When pressed for a reason, he said that their previous happiness had been a delusion— that Alys was too much like her mother. He had come to dislike all of Alys's relatives, but he particularly loathed Hannah and said that Alys reminded him of his mother-in-law in too many fatal ways.

In his old age, when Bertie had mellowed, he confessed that all of his other excuses for casting Alys aside were humbug. The real reason was his fickle nature. This did not make matters easier for Alys, who remained totally devoted to her husband. She persuaded Bertie to continue to live with her to carry on a common life of mutual interests and pursuits. From 1902 to 1911—when he finally forced Alys to agree to a separation—the estranged couple continued to live under the same roof.

Alys had a complete breakdown in 1902, and had several successive breakdowns in the subsequent years as she tried to win back his love. Once she even tried to commit suicide. There is not much doubt that the famous Lord Russell was cold and callous as far as his personal relations with women were concerned during his youth and middle-age.

Alys was so humiliated by her husband's alienation from her that she would not tell anybody, not even her mother. Hannah attributed her daughter's ill health to the fact that she had overextended herself trying to help others. During this traumatic period in her life, Alys, like Mary, often worried that her nervousness was inherited from Robert. Her mother disagreed. "I simply will not consent to thy thinking thee has inherited (Robert's) nervousness, for thine is an entirely different kind and quite to be accounted for by overwork."[2]

Some space has been taken to record the spiritual erosion taking place in the lives of Hannah's remaining children, simply to report the facts as they were. But these grand slides into unbelief were not the only facts. A captive of her ailing body, hemmed in by children who were cold to all she believed, Hannah now entered what was perhaps the most heroic period of her faith—and perhaps the most triumphant.

It is obvious where the eyes of her soul were set when Hannah wrote this note to Mary:

My darling Daughter,
    Thy letter . . . interests me very much. It shows that after all, your "top eyes" are not entirely closed, and your spirit is not altogether bound. . . . My soul was always so full of inspirations that a God was a necessity to me. I was like a bird, with an instinct of migration upon me, and a country to migrate to was as essential as it is to the bird. But you have seemed content to sit on a branch and merely flap the wings that were meant for flying, and to let your horizon be bounded by the fences of one little field, with no longing for the great spaces of the eternities. But thy letter gives a glimpse into other and higher needs of your nature, and I am delighted to see that you would like to fly, if you knew where the beautiful lands lie for which your spirit longs. I feel hopeful. . . .[3]

Hannah never would give up hope for her children. And

never would she stop declaring, as long as her tremorous hand could scratch words on a page, her utter hope in God and His goodness. Since she had retired from public work, she threw her remaining energies into writing. In late 1902, she was putting the finishing touches on her spiritual autobiography, which she titled *The Unselfishness of God and How I Discovered It*. That Hannah's faith remained steadfast is indicated in this statement to her friends:

> *It has been most interesting work, recalling all the various stages in my religious experience and recording the peaceful result of them all in my present quiet rest in the glorious salvation that is ours in the Lord Jesus Christ.*[4]

As a teenager, Karin was becoming quite deaf. There were operations and visits to ear specialists, all of which caused great consternation for Hannah. Ray was not quite as intelligent as Karin but was good at games, cheerful, and showed an early inclination to excel in leadership, which delighted her grandmother. She, like Hannah, was to become involved in public work, particularly in the struggle for women's rights.

In 1904, Hannah was mostly confined to a wheelchair. Since Ray and Karin were away at school, Mary, Logan, and Alys decided that their 74-year-old mother should not be living alone. The houses at Grosvenor Road and Friday's Hill were given up. Hannah lived in an apartment for two years, but in 1906 she and Logan settled in Iffley—a village near Oxford—in a pleasant house called Court Place, overlooking the Thames River.

Hannah became a renowned religious figure in her old age. Letters arrived from admirers all over the world, telling her how her books had changed their lives. Some of her followers were actually worshipful and described how they slept with her books under their pillows. They made pilgrimages to Iffley just to see the venerable old lady.

One woman, Mrs. W., arrived in 1908 and begged Logan for the merest glimpse of the face of the woman whom she had so admired for so many years. Hannah had developed such serious bladder trouble by that time that she tried to avoid callers. The worshipful lady was so insistent that Logan gave in.

Mrs. W. rushed into the room, knelt in front of Hannah's wheelchair, and burst into tears. Then, seizing Hannah's arthritic old hand in her own, she covered it with kisses. "To think that I should have this inestimable privilege!" she said over and over.

Logan was standing in the doorway, his mouth puckered, as if he had just eaten a lemon. The gushy scene was too much for him. He turned tail and fled.

Hannah, meanwhile, tried to extricate her hand from the moist kisses of the adoring lady. She was feeling anything but saintlike since her bladder was beginning to act up. Finally, Mrs. W. stood up dramatically, clasped her hands in front of her ample bosom, and gazed tearfully at Hannah. "I will treasure these moments all the rest of my life," she said, then turned and left.

Hannah, who never did know how to handle such hero worship, later commented, "The poor soul must have been sadly disappointed not to see my halo and wings!"[5]

By this stage of her life, Hannah saw no human being as saintly or sinless. She constantly warned against overpiousness, convinced that those who were put up on a spiritual pedestal nearly always fell off with a resounding crash. Much on her mind, of course, was what happened to her own husband Robert.

The unexpected period of peace after years of turmoil brought out a mischievous streak in Hannah. She said of her admiring correspondents: "I do wonder if a procession of all the people I have helped will come to greet me when I enter heaven! Or will they have discovered that I had everything wrong and only hindered them instead of helping and so come to try to persuade Peter to shut the gate against me!"[6]

In 1908, there was talk of her having an operation for her bladder trouble, although the doctors eventually decided against it. She wrote to Mary in Italy: *If I should die, which of course is always possible, I would like no weeping relatives to appear. I do not expect to make an edifying speech on my deathbed and I should far rather no one should "gather around" it.*[7]

―――――

During the whole last decade of her life, it is most important to note that Hannah continued to try to bring her children and grandchildren into a relationship with Jesus Christ. In letters to Mary, in particular, she made pointed comments about her own faith and how it had kept her going. In May 1910, she wrote Mary a passionate declaration of her love of Jesus. There was a wistful yearning in that letter, a plea that Mary would somehow find her way back to faith. Then in one of her last letters, written in a very shaky hand on April 22, 1911, she urged Mary to read the Bible for its literary merit, hoping by some circuitous method to interest her daughter again in Christianity. Almost with her last breath, she was trying to talk Mary into being a believer. Mary turned a deaf ear to all these appeals.

Hannah had become very frail by 1910 and was eagerly looking forward to her release. She had to sit in her wheelchair all day and all night. She even had to sleep sitting up, since she was unable to get into a bed. The year before, she had written to Mary, anticipating death and telling her with characteristic humor, *I have forbidden you to mourn for me. You are not to wear mourning, nor shed any tears or I will haunt you in the shape of a waterspout.*[8]

On Wednesday, April 27, 1911, Hannah had a slight stroke. Logan told her that he didn't think it was anything but an attack of indigestion. At this she turned on him quite fiercely and said, "Thee is not very encouraging, Logan."[9]

From some scribbled words, probably written by Mary on the back of a pamphlet, came these notations: *She died on May 1, 1911. She always said she would be "free to go" once Ray and Karin were grown up. Shortly before Mother died, Alys entered her room, her face bearing the marks of tears. "What is it, Alys? What did the doctor say?"*

Alys began to cry. "He says thee is losing thy hold on life, Mother."

"Oh, good!" she said—and then ceased to breathe.[10]

———

A recap of Hannah's children and grandchildren is sobering, from a spiritual viewpoint. After Hannah's death Mary continued to play her role in the glittering circle of artists and intellectuals who congregated around Florence, Italy. Bernhard Berenson was becoming famous and also financially comfortable. Mary was very much a part of his work. In between her hunts for obscure masterpieces and liaison work between Berenson and the American dealers who provided a market for the paintings they discovered, she had several love affairs. Her infidelities made her husband angry, but somehow they always managed to patch things up. She and B.B. led a life of emotional entanglements and upheavals. Mary died in March 1945.

Almost immediately after Hannah's death in May 1911, Bertie told Alys that he wanted a divorce. Alys agreed to a formal separation, still holding a forlorn hope that she and Bertie might get back together. Alys and Logan then set up housekeeping together, first at Ford Place in Sussex and later in a beautiful old Tudor farmhouse on the Solent River. A frustrated mother, Alys satisfied her maternal needs by filling her home every summer with numerous children of her friends and relatives. She remained devoted to Bertrand Russell all her life, although she finally agreed to a divorce in 1920. Alys died in 1951. Of the three, she was most like her mother—brave, kind, competent, and uncomplaining, though she too remained an unbeliever.

Logan became a writer and achieved a measure of literary success. His best known book was a collection of witty aphorisms named *Trivia and More Trivia*. He became manic-depressive in his old age—apparently he had inherited the family disease that was passed on to him from his father's side.

Soon after her grandmother's death, Ray married Oliver Strachey of the famous Strachey family. They had two children, Barbara, born in 1912, and Christopher, born in 1916. Ray was cheerful, independent, and enjoyed life. She wrote a number of books, including one called *The Cause*, on the women's movement in Great Britain. In 1918, when the Women's Suffrage Bill was passed, Ray was in the gallery of parliament: How altogether fitting and proper that the third generation of the fighting Whitall women should have been on the scene when the vote was given to women—a victory for which Hannah, Alys, and Ray had been fighting since the 1880s. Ray died following an operation in 1940 at the age of 53.[11]

Karin married Adrian Stephen, brother of the famous writer Virginia Woolf, in 1914. She and her husband entered medical school when they were in their thirties and became pioneers in psychiatry. The five-year medical course was especially difficult for Karin because of her deafness. At Cambridge University in 1911, she had won the first "star" of distinction in philosophy ever given to a woman as an undergraduate. She and Adrian had two children, Ann, born in 1916, and Judith, born in 1918. When Adrian died in 1948 following army service in World War II, Karin became a victim of that family disease of depression. Being a doctor, she began to slip unnoticed into overprescribing morphia for herself. In December 1953, she took a deliberate overdose.

Of Hannah's four great-grandchildren, Barbara Strachey would marry twice. She had a son, Roger, by her first husband. In 1984 she was a widow, still living in Oxford, England, enjoying an active life as a writer, traveler, and gourmet cook. By the time of the second edition of this book in 1993, she has been slowed down by health problems but still retains much of her old buoyancy. Christopher, a brilliant mathematician, made a name for himself in computers at Oxford and died in 1975. Ann and Judith Stephen both married and had numerous children. Ann became a doctor and is still living in England. Judith died in 1972.

This is Hannah's legacy, to all who recall her: She intensely loved her children and grandchildren, flaws and all. And they loved her, flaws and all. She ached when they did not accept her faith, but she loved them all regardless and prayed for them until the day she died. Who is to say that later generations will not benefit from her life of faithfulness and from her prayers?

Hannah's married life with Robert may seem strange to us today, but it was not so in the nineteenth century. People who fell out of love stayed married because of a sense of commitment and because it was the thing to do. They had seemed right for each other at the beginning. They did produce seven children. Their joint speaking and teaching ministry, brief as it was, indicated a spiritual compatibility. Nor was Robert a boorishly authoritarian husband.

But the question remains: What went wrong in this family, which boasted one of the leading spiritual voices of the last century? Digging into family records and archives turns up few clues. There might have been a misplaced gene in Robert that caused bouts of abnormal behavior and depression that was inherited by Logan, Alys, and their granddaughter Karin. There were obvious flaws in Robert's character.

But he was one of God's soldiers—a gifted teacher-preacher who led people to the Lord. Why would God let this happen to one of His own? How many times must Hannah have asked that question? Yet she never doubted Robert's eventual salvation.

And why didn't the Lord answer Hannah's prayers that her children become believers? Or her grandchildren? The person looking for fairness and justice in all of God's dealings with His children will be terribly upset by the returns Hannah Whitall Smith received for a lifetime of Christian service.

Was Hannah Whitall Smith bitter at the end?

Not in the least. She insisted her life had been blessed—and in many ways it was. She died quite peacefully, with total trust in her God.

To those countless Christians who today are trying to cling to belief although their lives are filled with pain, illness, disappointment, and heartbreak, Hannah would say: "Man's chief end is to glorify God and enjoy Him forever." He is not some kind of magic dispenser who exists only to give us what we think we need to make us happy.

Hannah's last book, *God of All Comfort*, refers to God's "shaking process." She wrote:

> *God's love for us is so great that when He sees His beloved ones becoming too secular or resting their souls on things that can be shaken, He sometimes removes those things from their lives in order that they may be driven to rest only on the things that cannot be shaken.*
>
> *The old mystics used to teach what they called "detachment," meaning the cutting loose of the soul from all that could hold it back from God. This need for "detachment" is the secret of many of our "shakings." We cannot follow the Lord fully so long as we are tied fast to anything else, anymore than a boat can sail out into the boundless ocean so long as it is tied fast to the shore.*
>
> *But we do not realize this and when the overturnings and shakings come, we are in despair and think we shall never reach the city that has foundations at all. But it is these very shakings that make it possible for us to reach it. The psalmist had learned this, and after all the shakings and emptyings of his eventual*

life, he cried, "My soul, wait thou only upon God; for my expectation is from Him. He only is my rock and my salvation; He is my defense; I shall not be moved. In God is my salvation and my glory: the rock of my strength, and my refuge, is in God" (Psalm 62:5–7).[11]

And so it was with Hannah—and can be for any of us, as she said:

When everything in our lives and experience is shaken that can be shaken, and only that which cannot be shaken remains, we are brought to see that God only is our rock and our foundation. Then we learn to have our expectation from Him alone.

In an introduction to the 1952 edition of *The Christian's Secret of a Happy Life,* the publishers spoke of Hannah Whitall Smith as being "a happy passenger in the Chariot of God, always in the van and never a despondent straggler in the rear. . . . Life to her was no dismal journey between the peaks of birth and death; it was the scene of a continuing triumphal entry into the courts of God."[12]

In one sense, this was true. Yet I'm convinced that few people in our time have had to face as many personal heartbreaks and disappointments as Hannah experienced.

The last chapter of *God of All Comfort* is titled "God Is Enough." In it she summed up her belief:

No soul can be really at rest until it has given up all dependence on everything else and has been forced to depend on the Lord alone. As long as our expectation is from other things, nothing but disappointment awaits us. Feelings may change, and will change, with our changing circumstances; doctrines and dogmas may be upset; Christian work may come to nought; prayers may seem to lose their fervency; promises may seem to fail; everything that we have believed in or depended upon may seem to be swept away, and only God is left, just God, the bare God, if I may be allowed the expression; simply and only God. . . .

This, then, is what I mean by God being enough. It is that we find in Him, the fact of His existence and of His character, all that we can possibly want for everything. God is, must be, our answer to every question and every cry of need. If there is any lack in the One who has undertaken to save us, nothing supplementary we can do will avail to make it up; and if there is no lack in Him, then He of himself and in himself is enough.

The all-sufficiency of God ought to be as complete to the child of God as the all-sufficiency of a good mother is to the child of that mother. We all know the utter rest of the little child in the mother's presence and the mother's love. That its mother is there is enough to make all fears and all troubles disappear. The child does not need the mother to make any promises; she herself, just as she is, without promises and without explanations, is all that the child needs. . . .

God's saints in all ages have known this and have realized that God was enough for them. Job said out of the depths of sorrow and trials, which few can equal, "Though he slay me, yet will I trust in him."

*Therefore, O doubting and sorrowful heart, cannot thee realize with Job and the saints of all ages that nothing else is needed to quiet all thy fears, but just this—*that God is.

God is enough! God is enough for time. God is enough for eternity. God is enough![13]

Explanation of Documentation:

All the dialogue scenes, narrative, quotes, and other personal material on Hannah Whitall Smith and her family were taken directly from her letters, her journals, family papers, and published material. The only exception was the scene in the last pages of Chapter Ten. This scene was based on informed guesswork rather than strict documentation. It is known that there was a final rift between Hannah and Robert that occurred around 1882–1883. Logan spoke of thirty years of congenial married life between his parents, although they were actually married forty-seven years. Walt Whitman, with the sensitivity of a poet, noticed some infelicity between Hannah and Robert between 1882 and 1888.* In his later years, Robert was unfaithful to his wife. No record survives of when this infidelity began. Therefore it seems logical to assume that Hannah discovered during 1882–1883 that Robert had taken up with another woman. I have included the scene at the end of Chapter Ten, placing the date at January 1, 1882, not only because that fitted in with Logan's dating, but also because Hannah's very poignant letter to Priscilla Mounsey seemed to correspond with the feelings she might have had upon discovering that Robert had been unfaithful to her.

Marie Henry

Remarkable Relations, pp. 73–74.

Time Line of Hannah Whitall Smith's Life

February 7, 1832
Hannah Whitall was born in Philadelphia, Pennsylvania, the oldest child of well-to-do Quaker parents, John Mickle Whitall and Mary Tatum Whitall. John Whitall was a former sea captain, owner of a prosperous glass works.

1833
Hannah's sister Sarah was born.

1834
Hannah's brother, James, was born.

1836
Hannah's younger sister, Mary, was born. (Mary married a doctor, James Thomas, and was the mother of pioneer educator, M. Carey Thomas. Hannah was very close to her two sisters. She and Mary and Sarah [Sally], along with a cousin, Carrie Lawrence, and a Mrs. Little referred to themselves as the "five birds" and confided and shared with one another throughout their lifetimes.)

1842–1848
Hannah was educated in various Friends' schools in Philadelphia.

1848–1851
Hannah taught geometry at one of the schools she had attended.

November 5, 1851
Hannah married Robert Pearsall Smith, a Philadelphia Quaker. Robert was a descendant of James Logan, William Penn's secretary. His people were very bookish, being publishers, printers, and librarians.

August 1852
A daughter, Nellie, was born to Hannah and Robert.

August 1854
A son, Frank, was born. He was a docile, tractable, serious-minded boy, a devout Christian.

1857
Martha Carey Thomas was born. She was Hannah's favorite niece and became the first woman president of Bryn Mawr College.

Christmas Day, 1857
Daughter Nellie died of bronchitis, age 5, the first of four children that Hannah and Robert lost through death.

1859
Robert and Hannah resigned from the Quaker Meeting due to the influence of Methodists. They were baptized. Robert became a Presbyterian and Hannah joined the Plymouth Brethren. They were banned from their parents' homes.

1864
Mary Pearsall Smith was born. That same year the family moved from Philadelphia to Millville, New Jersey, where the Whitall-Tatum Glass Works was located.

1865
(Lloyd) Logan Pearsall Smith was born.

1867
(Alice) Alys Pearsall Smith was born.

1868
(Rachel) Ray Pearsall Smith was born.

1869
The family moved back to Philadelphia. The Smiths and Whitalls had gotten over the horror of Robert and Hannah's leaving the Friends and were close again.

July 1872
Frank, age 18, died of typhoid fever.

1872–1873
Robert's second nervous breakdown. (The first one must have occurred in 1861 and was supposedly the result of a fall from a horse.) He "took the cure" at Clifton Springs, New York.

1873
Hannah's youngest child died in infancy.

Summer 1874
Hannah traveled to England. She and Robert conducted evangelistic meetings at homes of British aristocrats.

1875
Robert's triumphant series of evangelistic meetings in Europe, culminating in meetings in Brighton, England, in June. Publication date of *The Christian's Secret of a Happy Life*.

June 1875
The scandal that ruined Robert's ministry became public in England.

Summer 1875
Robert was in disgrace. The Smiths went back to Philadelphia.

1875–1876
Robert's third nervous breakdown. He began to lose his faith.

June 1877
Hannah's father, John Mickle Whitall, died.

1877–1884
The Smiths took summer trips to scenic spots in the U.S., camping out. They visited Yellowstone, Yosemite, the Adirondacks, and Maine.

January 1880
Hannah's mother, Mary Tatum Whitall, died.

February 1880
Ray (youngest child of Robert and Hannah) died, age 11, of scarlet fever.

1880–1900
Hannah became a public figure. She traveled and spoke at W.C.T.U. meetings and campaigns for women's suffrage.

1883
Mary, age 19, attended Smith College. She began to lose her faith.

1885
Mary attended Harvard Annex (later known as Radcliffe). Logan attended Harvard. Mary fell in love with a Roman Catholic Irish barrister (lawyer) named Frank Costelloe. The family traveled to Europe in the summer. Mary and Frank were married in Oxford, England, in September.
February 18, 1886
Hannah's sister, Sarah (Whitall) Nicholson, died, age 52.
June 4, 1887
(Rachel) Ray Costelloe born to Frank and Mary.
1887
Logan, age 22, gave up working for the family glass business and decided to pursue a literary career.
1888
Hannah's last surviving sister, Mary (Whitall) Thomas, died in July of breast cancer. The Pearsall Smith family moved to England, leased a house in London, 44 Grosvenor Road, four doors away from the house where Frank and Mary Costelloe lived. Alys was still in the U.S., in college at Bryn Mawr. Logan enrolled at Oxford.
March 1889
Catherine Elizabeth Costelloe (called Karin) was born.
1889
The family leased a summer place in Sussex called Friday's Hill. It became a gathering place for various American and British intellectuals during the 1890s. Friends of Mary, Logan, and Alys met there to solve the problems of the world. They included Beatrice and Sidney Webb, George Santayana, Roger Fry, Bertrand Russell, Bernhard Berenson, and George Bernard Shaw.
1889–1890
Mary became disillusioned with her marriage with Frank and suffered a partial breakdown. Bernhard Berenson showed up at Friday's Hill.
1891
Mary left Frank and the two little girls, ages two and four, and went off to Italy to "study art" with Bernhard Berenson.
1894
Alys and Bertrand Russell were courting. Alys, age 27, and Bertrand, age 22, were married in December.

April, 1898
Robert was "safely gathered."
December 1899
Frank Costelloe died of cancer of the ear.
1900
Court battle for custody of the grandchildren. In December, Bernhard Berenson and Mary were married.
1902
Bertrand Russell told Alys he "didn't love her anymore." Alys suffered a breakdown, but was so close-mouthed about her marriage that Hannah thought the illness was caused by overwork.
1903
The Unselfishness of God, Hannah's spiritual autobiography, was published. She was increasingly crippled with arthritis.
1904
Hannah, Ray, and Karin moved from the house on Grosvenor Road to a new flat in London.
1906
God of All Comfort (Living in the Sunshine) was published. This was Hannah's last book. She was immobilized by arthritis or rheumatism by that time, and suffered from shingles and bladder problems. She moved to the village of Iffley, near Oxford, to live with her bachelor son, Logan, age 41.
May 1, 1911
Hannah was "safely gathered."

Endnotes

Chapter 1

1. H.W.S. (Hannah Whitall Smith), *The Unselfishness of God and How I Discovered It* (New York: Fleming H. Revell Co., 1903), pp. 106–109.
2. Smith Archive, Oxford, England (in the keeping of Barbara Strachey Halpern), Journal of H.W.S., Volume II (1849, April 3, 1849).
3. *The Unselfishness of God*, p. 133.
4. Journal, Volume II.
5. Smith Archive, Letters of H.W.S., Letter to cousin Carrie (February 17, 1850), p. 4.
6. Journal, Volume V (April 7, 1851).
7. Journal, Volume V (June 16, 1851).

Chapter 2

1. Smith Archive, Journal of H.W.S., Volume VI (1851–1856; July 22, 1852).
2. Journal, Volume VI (November 7, 1855).
3. Journal, Volume VI (December 6, 1852; November 5, 1855), Volume VII (March 16, 1857).
4. Journal, Volume VII (December 28, 1857).
5. Journal, Volume VII (December 28, 1857).

6. Journal, Volume VIII (February 2, 1858).
7. Journal, Volume VII (December 30, 1857).
8. Journal, Volume VIII (September 2, 1858).

Chapter 3

1. *The Unselfishness of God*, p. 82.
2. Smith Archive, Journal of H.W.S., Volume VIII (January 31, 1859).
3. Journal, Volume VIII (September 25, 1859), and Smith Archive, Letters to H.W.S., Letter to sister Sally (October 30, 1859).
4. Letters of H.W.S., Letter to sister Sally (October 30, 1859).

Chapter 4

1. *The Unselfishness of God*, pp. 195–196.
2. Ibid., p. 201.
3. Ibid., pp. 205–206 (pronouns changed).
4. *The God of All Comfort*, 1956 edition (Chicago: Moody Press), pp. 12–13; p. 210 (pronouns changed).
5. *The Unselfishness of God*, pp. 218–219.
6. Ibid., pp. 218–219.

Chapter 5

1. Smith Archive, Journal of H.W.S., Volume VIII (Atlantic City, August 1861).
2. Smith Archive, Letters of H.W.S., Letter to sister Mary (February 28, 1864).
3. Letters of H.W.S., Letter to mother-in-law (June 7, 1864).
4. *The Unselfishness of God*, pp. 238–245.
5. Ibid., pp. 288–289.
6. Smith Archive, Journal of H.W.S., Volume X (June 10, 1869).
7. Ibid., p. 288.

Chapter 6

1. Smith Archive, Letters of H.W.S., Letters to friend (August 15, 1872).
2. Letters of H.W.S., Letter to Anna Shipley (August 24, 1872).
3. Letters of H.W.S., Letter to R.P.S. (Robert Pearsall Smith), (November 3, 1873).

4. Letters of H.W.S., Letter to sister Sally (July 14, 1873).
5. Letters of H.W.S., Letter to R.P.S. (June 22, 1873).
6. Letters of H.W.S., Letter to R.P.S. (July 4, 1873).
7. Letters of H.W.S., Letter to R.P.S. (July 7, 1873).
8. Letters of H.W.S., Letter to cousin Carrie (August 8, 1873).
9. Letters of H.W.S., Letter to cousin Carrie (August 30, 1873).

Chapter 7

1. *The Unselfishness of God*, pp. 205, 260.
2. Barbara Strachey, *Remarkable Relations* (London: Victor Gollancz, Ltd., 1980), pp. 41–42.
3. Smith Archive, Unpublished manuscript by Ray Strachey, Chapter 3, p. 4.
4. Smith Archive, Letters of H.W.S., Letter to Mrs. Beck (September 24, 1874).
5. Letters of H.W.S., Letter to R.P.S. (December 8, 1873).
6. Letters of H.W.S., Letter to R.P.S. (March 7, 1875).
7. Letters of H.W.S., Letter to R.P.S. (March 27, 1875).
8. Letters of H.W.S., Letter to R.P.S. (March 7, 1875).
9. Letters of H.W.S., Letter to R.P.S. (April 17, 1875).
10. Letters of H.W.S., Letter to sister (May 23, 1875).
11. *Hannah Whitall Smith: Religious Fanaticism*, Edited with an introduction by Ray Strachey (London: Faber & Twyer, Ltd., 1927), pp. 251–252.
11. Smith Archive, Unpublished manuscript by Ray Strachey, Chapter 3, p. 2.
12. Unpublished manuscript, Chapter 3, pp. 12–13.

Chapter 8

1. Smith Archive, Letters of H.W.S., Letter to Mrs. Beck (July 7, 1875), *Remarkable Relations*, p. 46.
2. Letters of H.W.S., Letter to Mrs. Beck (July 7, 1875).
3. Smith Archive, Unpublished manuscript by Ray Strachey, Chapter 3, p. 14.
4. Letters of H.W.S., Letter to friend (July 7, 1875).
5. *Remarkable Relations*, Chapter 3, p. 48.
6. Ibid., Chapter 4, p. 50.
7. Hannah Whitall Smith, *The Christian's Secret of a Happy Life* (Old Tappan, New Jersey: Fleming H. Revell Company, 1952; originally published in 1875), Chapter 12, p. 149.

8. Letters of H.W.S., Letter to R.P.S. (June 5, 1877).
9. Letters of H.W.S., Letter to R.P.S. (June 20, 1877).
10. Letters of H.W.S., Letter to R.P.S. (June 20, 1877).
11. Letters of H.W.S., Letter to R.P.S. (June 20, 1877).
12. Letters of H.W.S., Letter to R.P.S. (May 31, 1877).
13. Letters of H.W.S., Letter to Anna (May 20, 1878).

Chapter 9

1. *Philadelphia Quaker*, p. 41.
2. Ibid., p. 46.
3. Ibid., pp. 57–59.
4. Smith Archive, Letters of H.W.S., Letter to R.P.S. (August 9–11, 1883).
5. *Philadelphia Quaker*, pp. 67–68.
6. Letters of H.W.S., Circular letter (January 26, 1889).

Chapter 10

1. Smith Archive, Letters of H.W.S., Letter to Mrs. Wilson (July 2, 1877).
2. Letters of H.W.S., Letter to mother (June 10, 1878).
3. Letters of H.W.S., Letter to Anna (February 9, 1880).
4. Smith Archive, Journal of H.W.S., Volume X (December 30, 1880).
5. Letters of H.W.S., Letter to Anna (February 9, 1880).
6. Letters of H.W.S., Letter to sister Sally (September 2, 1880).
7. Letters of H.W.S., Letter to R.P.S. (April 16, 1878).
8. Letters of H.W.S., Letter to Priscilla Mounsey (January 1, 1882).

Chapter 11

1. Helen Whitall (Thomas) Flexner, *A Quaker Childhood* (New Haven, Conn.: Yale University Press, 1940), pp. 86–87.
2. Smith Archive, Letters of H.W.S., Letter to R.P.S. (April 1877).

Chapter 12

1. Smith Archive, Letters of H.W.S., Letter to Anna (September 3, 1884).
2. Letters of H.W.S., Letter to Carrie (February 22, 1880).

3. Letters of H.W.S., Letter to daughter Mary (November 14, 1883).

4. *Hannah Whitall Smith, Philadelphia Quaker,* Edited by her son Logan Pearsall Smith (New York: Harcourt, Brace and Company, 1950), p. 65.

5. Letters of H.W.S., Letter to daughter Mary (January 27, 1883).

6. Letters of H.W.S., Letter to daughter Mary (February 7, 1883).

7. Letters of H.W.S., Letter to Mr. Palmer (1884).

8. Letters of H.W.S., Letters to daughter Mary (January 20, 1885; January 23, 1885; February 24, 1885; March 11, 1885; March 14, 1885).

9. Letters of H.W.S., Letter to daughter Mary (September 19, 1910).

10. Letters of H.W.S., Letters to daughter Mary (January 20, 1885; January 23, 1885; February 24, 1885; March 11, 1885; March 14, 1885).

11. Letters of H.W.S., Letter to Priscilla Mounsey (May 29, 1885).

12. Letters of H.W.S., Letter to daughter Mary (March 4, 1885).

13. Letters of H.W.S., Letter to daughter Mary (September 13, 1885).

Chapter 13

1. *Remarkable Relations*, p. 111.

2. Ibid., p. 114.

3. Ibid., p. 117.

4. Letters of H.W.S., Letter to daughter Mary (November 1892).

5. Letters of H.W.S., Letter to daughter Mary (October 17, 1892).

6. Letters of H.W.S., Letter to daughter Mary (January 13, 1893).

7. Letters of H.W.S., Letter to daughter Mary (January 13, 1893; January 17, 1893).

8. Letters of H.W.S., Letter to daughter Mary (March 21, 1893).

9. *The Unselfishness of God*, pp. 298–299.

Chapter 14

1. *Remarkable Relations*, p. 127.

2. Ibid., p. 106.

3. Ibid., p. 135.

4. Smith Archive, Letters of H.W.S., Letter to daughter Mary (April 26, 1894).

5. Letters of H.W.S., Letter to daughter Mary (April 26, 1894).

6. *Remarkable Relations*, pp. 137–144.
7. Letters of H.W.S., Letter to Alys (February 14, 1895).
8. Letters of H.W.S., Letter to Alys (February 14, 1895).

Chapter 15

1. Rachel (Ray) Costelloe Strachey, *A Quaker Grandmother* (New York: Fleming H. Revell Co., 1914), pp. 22–23.
2. Letters of H.W.S., Letter to friends (June 3, 1895).
3. Smith Archive, Unpublished manuscript by Ray Strachey, Chapter 6, p. 4.

Chapter 16

1. Smith Archive, Letters of H.W.S., Letters to Alys (January 28, 1895).
2. Letters of H.W.S., Letter to Alys (February 2, 1895).
3. *Remarkable Relations*, p. 187.
4. Letters of H.W.S., Letter to friend (April 30, 1898).
5. Letters of H.W.S., Circular letter (December 20, 1900).
6. Letters of H.W.S., Circular letter (December 20, 1900).
7. *Remarkable Relations*, p. 193.
8. Letters of H.W.S., Circular letter (December 20, 1900).
9. Letters of H.W.S., Letter to daughter Mary (November 6, 1904).
10. Hannah Whitall Smith, *Everyday Religion* (Chicago: Moody Press, 1966; originally published by Fleming H. Revell in 1893), p. 90.

Chapter 17

1. *Philadelphia Quaker*, pp. 139–140.
2. Smith Archive, Letters of H.W.S., Letter to Alys (May 17, 1902).
3. Letters of H.W.S., Letter to Mary (February 16, 1902).
4. Letters of H.W.S., Circular letter (November 3, 1902).
5. Letters of H.W.S., Letter to daughter Mary (February 6, 1908).
6. Letters of H.W.S., Letter to daughter Mary (February 5, 1906).
7. Letters of H.W.S., Letter to daughter Mary (November 13, 1908).
8. Letters of H.W.S., Letter to daughter Mary (April 22, 1911).
9. *Remarkable Relations*, p. 256.

10. Smith Archive, Family Documents.
11. Hannah Whitall Smith, *God of All Comfort* (Chicago: Moody Press, 1956; originally published as *Living in the Sunshine* by Fleming H. Revell in 1906), pp. 150, 151, 154, 157, 158.
12. *The Christian's Secret of a Happy Life*, pp. 7–8.
13. *God of All Comfort*, pp. 243, 246, 249, 252, 253.

Bibliography

Flexner, Helen Whitall (Thomas). *A Quaker Childhood.* New Haven, Conn.: Yale University Press, 1940.

Hardy, Robert Gathorne. *Recollections of Logan Pearsall Smith: The Story of a Friendship.* New York: The Macmillan Co., 1950.

Parker, Robert Allerton. *The Transatlantic Smiths.* New York: Random House, 1959.

Russell, Bertrand. *The Autobiography of Bertrand Russell* (three volumes). Boston: Little, Brown, 1967.

Secrest, Meryle. *Being Bernhard Berenson,* a biography. New York: Holt, Rinehart & Winston, 1979.

Smith, Hannah Whitall. *Child Culture or the Science of Motherhood.* New York: Fleming H. Revell Co., 1894.

———. *The Christian's Secret of a Happy Life.* Old Tappan, N.J.: Fleming H. Revell Co., 1952. (Originally published by Fleming H. Revell in 1875.)

———. *Everyday Religion.* Chicago: Moody Press, 1966. (Originally published by Fleming H. Revell in 1893.)

———. *God of All Comfort.* Chicago: Moody Press, 1956. (Originally published as *Living in the Sunshine* by Fleming H. Revell in 1906.)

————. *Philadelphia Quaker: The Letters of Hannah Whitall Smith.* Edited by her son Logan Pearsall Smith, with a bibliographical preface by Robert Gathorne Hardy. New York: Harcourt Brace & Co., Inc., 1950.

————. *Religious Fanaticism: Extracts from the Papers of Hannah Whitall Smith.* Edited with an introduction by Ray Strachey. London: Faber and Gwyer, Ltd., 1928.

————. *The Unselfishness of God and How I Discovered It: My Spiritual Autobiography.* New York: Fleming H. Revell Co., 1903.

Smith, Logan Pearsall. *Unforgotten Years.* Boston: Little, Brown, 1939.

Sprigge, Sylvia. *Berenson: A Biography.* London: George Allen & Unwin, Ltd., Ruskin House, 1960.

Strachey, Barbara. *Remarkable Relations.* London: Victor Gollancz, Ltd., 1981.

Strachey, Rachel (Ray Costelloe). *The Cause: A Short History of the Women's Movement in Great Britain.* London: G. Bell & Sons, Ltd., 1928.

————. *A Quaker Grandmother.* New York: Fleming H. Revell Co., 1914.

————. *Shaken by the Wind: A Story of Fanaticism.* New York: The Macmillan Co., 1928.

Warfield, Benjamin Breckenridge. *Perfectionism.* Oxford: Oxford University Press, 1931.

Webb, Beatrice and Sidney. *The Letters of Beatrice and Sidney Webb.* Volume I: Apprenticeships, 1873–1892; and Volume II: Our Partnership, 1892–1912. Edited by Norman McKenzie. Cambridge: Cambridge University Press, 1978.

Willard, Frances E. *Women and Temperance, or, The Work and Workers of the Women's Christian Temperance Union.* Hartford, Conn.: Park Publishing Co., 1883.